Partners in Life and Love

*A Preparation Handbook for the
Celebration of Catholic Marriage
with Readings from the New Lectionary*

JOSEPH R. GIANDURCO AND JOHN S. BONNICI

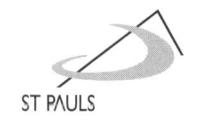

ST PAULS

Library of Congress Cataloging-in-Publication Data

Giandurco, Joseph R.
    Partners in life and love: a preparation handbook for the
celebration of Catholic marriage / Joseph R. Giandurco and John
Bonnici.
      p.   cm.
Includes bibliographical references.
ISBN 0-8189-0934-X
1. Marriage — Religious aspects — Catholic Church. 2. Marriage
service. 3. Catholic Church — Liturgy — Texts. I. Bonnici, John.
II. Title.
BX2250.G53   1996
   264'.02085 — dc20   96-22274
                                 CIP

Nihil Obstat:	Imprimatur:
Francis J. McAree, STD	✠ Patrick Sheridan, DD
Censor Librorum	Vicar General, Archdiocese of New York
	September 4, 1996

Scripture selections are taken from the Lectionary for Mass for use in the Dioceses of the United States of America, second typical edition. Copyright © 1970, 1986, 1992, 1998, 2001 Confraternity of Christian Doctrine, Inc., Washington, D.C. All rights reserved. No part of this work may be reproduced or transmitted in any form or by any means, electronic or mechanical, including photocopying, recording, or by any information storage and retrieval system, without permission in writing from the copyright owner.

The English translation of the General Introduction, some Psalm responses, some Alleluia and Gospel verses, and the Lenten Gospel Acclamations, some Summaries, and the Titles and Conclusion of the Readings, from the *Lectionary for Mass* © 1968, 1981, 1997, International Committee on English in the Liturgy, Inc., Washington, D.C. All rights reserved.

The English translation of the ritual texts from Rite of Marriage © 1969, International Committee on English in the Liturgy, Inc. All rights reserved.

Excerpts from the English translation of the *Catechism of the Catholic Church* for use in the United States of America Copyright © 1994, United States Catholic Conference, Inc. — Libreria Editrice Vaticana. Used with permission.

English translation of the *Catechism of the Catholic Church: Modifications from the* Editio Typica Copyright © 1997 Libreria Editrice Vaticana — United States Catholic Conference, Inc. Used with permission.

Produced and designed in the United States of America by the
Fathers and Brothers of the Society of St. Paul,
2187 Victory Boulevard, Staten Island, New York 10314,
as part of their communications apostolate.

ISBN 10: 0-8189-0934-X
ISBN 13: 978-0-8189-0934-4

Printing Information:

Current Printing - first digit		8	9	10	11	12
Year of Current Printing - first year shown				2009		2010

Preface

John Cardinal O'Connor

For my entire life as a priest of more than fifty years, I have preferred to meet personally with couples who wish to enter into a Catholic marriage, and to hold an extended series of discussions with them. This has been true whether both parties are Catholic or one is of a different faith.

While I support and have participated in various kinds of group sessions, such as "Pre-Cana Conferences", I never feel fully satisfied, even today, to settle for such sessions alone. Even as Archbishop of New York I have tried to engage a couple face-to-face for as long as they may seem to need. That such an approach is extremely time-consuming is obvious. But how many other things do we do that are more important than trying to help people enter into and sustain good, permanent marriages? Generations may depend on one marriage. Children are profoundly affected. All society is ultimately at stake.

Sadly, many who accept that it takes years to become a priest, a doctor, a lawyer, seem to take success in marriage and in rearing children as the easiest things in the world. Yet how many couples entering into marriage starry-eyed and romantic, convinced that "love" takes care of everything, find themselves confronted in short order with the realities of married life for which they are totally unprepared?

Partners in Life and Love is overdue. While many fine materials are already available for use by and with those preparing to celebrate a Catholic marriage, this work offers certain particularly helpful features. In addition to sections included in a number of manuals, such as helps for planning the liturgy, selecting from a number of scriptural readings and understanding the marriage rite itself, *Partners in Life and Love* includes a readily readable approach to an understanding of the theological and scriptural underpinnings of marriage, as well as of the canonical requirements of this very special sacrament.

This is a manual that may be profitably used both by couples themselves and by priests assisting them to prepare for marriage. It will prove useful in both group and individual sessions. And speaking from a thoroughly selfish viewpoint, I am happy to say that I expect it to be exceptionally useful to me as I continue my lifelong efforts to help couples make their marriages everything God wills, all they personally hope for and what society desperately needs.

John Cardinal O'Connor
Archbishop of New York

Biblical Abbreviations

OLD TESTAMENT

Genesis	Gn	Nehemiah	Ne	Baruch	Ba
Exodus	Ex	Tobit	Tb	Ezekiel	Ezk
Leviticus	Lv	Judith	Jdt	Daniel	Dn
Numbers	Nb	Esther	Est	Hosea	Ho
Deuteronomy	Dt	1 Maccabees	1 M	Joel	Jl
Joshua	Jos	2 Maccabees	2 M	Amos	Am
Judges	Jg	Job	Jb	Obadiah	Ob
Ruth	Rt	Psalms	Ps	Jonah	Jon
1 Samuel	1 S	Proverbs	Pr	Micah	Mi
2 Samuel	2 S	Ecclesiastes	Ec	Nahum	Na
1 Kings	1 K	Song of Songs	Sg	Habakkuk	Hab
2 Kings	2 K	Wisdom	Ws	Zephaniah	Zp
1 Chronicles	1 Ch	Sirach	Si	Haggai	Hg
2 Chronicles	2 Ch	Isaiah	Is	Malachi	Ml
Ezra	Ezr	Jeremiah	Jr	Zechariah	Zc
		Lamentations	Lm		

NEW TESTAMENT

Matthew	Mt	Ephesians	Eph	Hebrews	Heb
Mark	Mk	Philippians	Ph	James	Jm
Luke	Lk	Colossians	Col	1 Peter	1 P
John	Jn	1 Thessalonians	1 Th	2 Peter	2 P
Acts	Ac	2 Thessalonians	2 Th	1 John	1 Jn
Romans	Rm	1 Timothy	1 Tm	2 John	2 Jn
1 Corinthians	1 Cor	2 Timothy	2 Tm	3 John	3 Jn
2 Corinthians	2 Cor	Titus	Tt	Jude	Jude
Galatians	Gal	Philemon	Phm	Revelation	Rv

Document Abbreviations

FC   Familiaris Consortio (Apostolic Exhortation on the Family)

GS   Gaudium et Spes (Pastoral Constitution on the Church in the Modern World)

EV   Evangelium Vitae (The Gospel of Life)

How to Use This Book

This book is designed to help you prepare for your wedding liturgy, and to give you an introduction to the Church's teachings on the Sacrament of Marriage.

1. Using this book to plan your wedding.

The Church is happy to offer you the chance to work together with your priest or deacon to plan your wedding ceremony. You can select from a number of scripture readings, prayers and blessings, as well as the words you will use to marry each other. You should use these choices to express to yourselves and to the Church community your love and commitment in the Sacrament of Marriage.

The rite of marriage should ordinarily be held within a Mass, where it is combined with the usual order of prayers and readings. If you and your priest or deacon decide to hold your wedding outside of the Mass, there is a separate rite, but it will follow the same basic pattern. The following outline will help you see the elements of the rite.

In the outline, the bold print shows where you can make selections in the rite. The choices can be found on the pages indicated. After you have made each choice, write it in the detachable Liturgy Planner at the back of this book. You should bring this book and the Planner when you meet with your priest or deacon to discuss your wedding ceremony.

Marriage Rite During Mass

Introductory Rites
Greeting
Penitential Rite
Gloria
Opening Prayer (see pages 34-35)
Liturgy of the Word
**Old Testament Reading
(see pages 36-43)**

Responsorial Psalm (see pages 44-49)
**New Testament Reading
(see pages 50-62)**
Alleluia Verse (see page 63)
Gospel Reading (see pages 64-70)
Homily
Rite of Marriage
Questions to the Couple

The Giving of Consent (Vows)
(see pages 72-74)
Blessing of the Rings
(see pages 74-75)
Exchange of Rings
Prayer of the Faithful (see pages 75-77)
Liturgy of the Eucharist
Presentation of the Gifts
Prayer Over the Gifts (see page 78)
Eucharistic Prayer
Communion Rite

Lord's Prayer
Nuptial Blessing (see pages 80-83)
Sign of Peace
Breaking of the Bread
Communion (see pages 83-84)
Special Devotions
(see page 86)
Prayer After Communion
(see pages 86-87)
Blessing (see pages 87-89)
Dismissal

2. Using this book to learn about the Church's teachings.

This book contains a brief presentation of the Church's teachings on marriage. Using the *Catechism of the Catholic Church* as its guide, it sets forth the People of God's understanding of the sacrament throughout history. The essay explains some of the laws of the Church, in an effort to anticipate some of the most common questions that arise in the time before the wedding. It also summarizes Catholic moral teachings about marriage and sexuality, so that you may have a clear and faithful presentation of these important principles. We strongly encourage you to read this essay, because we believe it will deepen your awareness and appreciation of the blessings God will give to you through the grace of the sacrament.

In the back of this book, you will find a suggested reading list. Some of the books will help you to a greater understanding of the teachings of the Church on marriage. We especially recommend the works of Pope John Paul II, who is a great friend and advocate for married couples and families. "Do not be afraid," as His Holiness himself says — his writings on marriage and the family are very readable, and are not only for experts or theologians. We also urge you to include in your family library a copy of the *Catechism of the Catholic Church* — a clear and complete presentation of the Church's teachings. Other books on the list offer some basic skills to strengthen your relationship. All of these have been helpful to many marriages, and we hope they will give you the same benefits.

Gene Plaisted, OSC

HOLY MATRIMONY

Catholic Teaching on the Sacrament of Marriage

I. Marriage as a Covenant

In recent years the Church's attitude toward the celebration of marriage and married life has shown a renewed understanding and appreciation of revealed truth. Catholic teaching identifies marriage as a unique institution. Recognizing the rich and vibrant Judeo-Christian tradition surrounding the union of husband and wife, the Church declares that, "The matrimonial covenant, by which a man and a woman establish between themselves a partnership of the whole of life, is by its nature ordered toward the good of the spouses and the procreation and education of offspring; this covenant between baptized persons has been raised by Christ the Lord to the dignity of a sacrament" (Code of Canon Law, Canon 1055, par.1).

This definition of the Sacrament of Matrimony is the culmination of a long and dynamic history. The teaching of the Church on the institution of marriage is rooted in the history of salvation. From covenant to sacrament, matrimony is the realization of love. Our reflection, however, begins with the universal character of marriage itself.

A. A Universal Phenomenon

In his Apostolic Exhortation on the Family (*Familiaris Consortio*), Pope John Paul II locates the plan of God for marriage and the family in love. He writes, "God is love and in himself he lives a mystery of personal loving communion. Creating the human race in his own image and continually keeping it in being, God inscribed in the humanity of man and woman the vocation, and thus the capacity and responsibility of love and communion. Love is therefore the fundamental and innate vocation of every human being" (*FC* 11). Marriage is thus a realization of the vocation to love.

A common nature and the mutual capacity to love shared by all men and women marks the institution of marriage as a universal phenomenon. Despite differences of culture, society and religious perspective, marriage is able to maintain a number of steadfast and common attributes. According to the *Catechism*, "These differences should not cause us to forget its common and permanent characteristics" (*Catechism* 1603). The institution of marriage is not limited to a specific culture, social system or religious faith. Authentic expressions of matrimony are the fulfillment of an innate capacity that is common to human nature. The common denominator is the gift of love.

This realization, however, is not always complete. Despite hard work and good intentions, the full truth of married love is not evident by human means alone. Instead, the true nature of love is discovered in God. For the Christian, the bond of marriage finds its beginning in Divine Revelation. In God's plan, marriage is able to transcend the mere contract. The fulfillment of the human capacity to love in marriage is expressed in the form of a covenant. This expression was clearly present for the people of Israel.

B. More than a Contract

Like their neighboring cultures, the people of Israel recognized the bond of marriage as a human institution. Initially, the rite of matrimony was understood as a form of security. The legal union of man and woman was viewed as a means of insuring order, stability and the continuation of a family line. References in scripture to laws and regulations regarding marriage underscore the importance of a good and solid married life (cf. Dt 22:13-29 and 2 S 12:1-13).

To Israel, however, marriage was not limited to the legal institution alone. In the Old Testament, the marriage partnership is revealed in the creation account. Both creation narratives (Gn 1-2) emphasize the unity and blessedness of marriage.

The people of Israel are the chosen people of God. The existence of man and woman is not accidental. The human person is created in the image and likeness of God. "God created man in his image; in the divine image he created him; male and female he created them" (Gn 1:27). Moreover, the union of man and woman is a dynamic continuation of this creative act. The love shared between husband and wife is gradually transformed into a symbol of God's love for his people. "Since God created him man and woman, their mutual love becomes an image of the absolute and unfailing love with which God loves man" (*Catechism* 1604). For the people of Israel, married love and the love of God are brought together in the reality of a covenant.

The idea of covenant was not foreign to the mind and heart of the Israelite community. For Israel, God and his people formed a community of life and salvation. This relationship is personal. Speaking directly to the People of God, the book of Deuteronomy declares: "Today you are making this agreement with the Lord: he is to be your God and you are to walk in his ways and observe his statutes, commandments and decrees, and to hearken to his voice" (Dt 26:17). Consequently, "he will then raise you high in praise and renown and glory above all other nations he has made, and you will be a people sacred to the LORD, your God as he promised" (Dt 26:19). Israel is consecrated to God in a special relationship. Moreover, the covenant of God with his people was marked by a love that is unified, exclusive, faithful and indissoluble.

Over the course of time, the Old Testament understanding of marriage changed. The notion of contract was gradually replaced by a more powerful and personal image. On the one hand the covenant shared by God and his people was expressed, reflected and understood in the inter-personal bond of marriage. On the other hand, the reality of marriage itself was identified and defined by the faithful love of God pledged to the people of Israel. This dynamic was actively present in the call of the Jewish prophets. In fact, "Seeing God's covenant with Israel in the image of exclusive and faithful married love, the prophets prepared the Chosen People's conscience for a deepened understanding of the unity and indissolubility of marriage" (*Catechism* 1611; cf. Ho 1-3; Is 54;62; Jr 2-3;31; Ezk 16;23; Ml 2:13-17). The second chapter of the book of Jeremiah is a good example of this. In the voice of the prophet, the Lord exclaims, "I remember the devotion of your youth, how you loved me as a bride, Following me in the desert, in a land unsown" (Jr 2:2).

For the Israelite community, God's love for his people is unquestionably faithful and true. The loving relationship shared by a husband and wife was understood in the same context. Beyond the confines of a legal contract, the love of marriage was recognized as a true covenant. In the Old Testament, faithfulness in marriage and fidelity to the covenant were intimately linked. According to John Paul II, "The communion of love between God and people, a fundamental part of the Revelation and faith experience of Israel, find a meaningful expression in the marriage covenant which is established between a man and a woman" (*FC* 12).

C. *A Partnership of Life and Love*

As a covenant, the loving union of husband and wife is created and sustained by God. Like God's relationship to the people of Israel, the union of man and woman is a true partnership. After commenting on man as the image of God, the Fathers of the Second Vatican Council remind the faithful that "God did not create man a solitary being. From the beginning 'male and female he created them' (Gn 1:27). This partnership of man and woman constitutes the first form of communion between persons" (*GS* 12).

The partnership of marriage is neither temporary nor static. Reflecting the covenant shared between God and Israel, the union of man and woman is indissoluble. "The intimate partnership of life and the love which constitutes the married state has been established by the creator and endowed by him with its own proper laws: it is rooted in the contract of its partners, that is, in their irrevocable consent" (*GS* 48). The partnership of marriage is not an individual affair. Like the nature of a true partnership, both husband and wife are called to actively love one another in God. Moreover, the couple "help and serve each other by their marriage partnership; they become conscious of their unity and experience it more deeply from day to day" (*GS* 48).

In addition to demonstrating that marriage is a true partnership dedicated to life and love, the story of creation teaches us that husband and wife complement each other.

D. Husband and Wife Complement Each Other

The creation event culminated with the presence of the human person. Following the creation of heaven and earth, "The LORD God formed man out of the clay of the ground and blew into his nostrils the breath of life, and so man became a living being" (Gn 2:7). Solitary man, however, was not complete. For God, "it is not good for the man to be alone" (Gn 2:18). It is the creation of another human person — the woman — equal yet different, that brings the creation account to a close: "So the LORD God cast a deep sleep on the man, and while he was asleep, he took out one of his ribs and closed up its place with flesh. The LORD God then built up into a woman the rib that he had taken from the man" (Gn 2:21-22). Interpreting the significance of this text, the *Catechism* writes: "The woman, 'flesh of his flesh,' his equal, his nearest in all things, is given to him by God as a 'helpmate'; she thus represents God from whom comes our help" (*Catechism* 1605; cf. Gn 2:18-25).

The created relationship of man and woman is not antagonistic, servile, or instrumental. Rather, man and woman are called to lovingly complement one another. Pope John Paul II writes: "Above all it is important to underline the equal dignity and responsibility of women with men. This equality is realized in a unique manner in that reciprocal self-giving by each one to the other and by both to the children which is proper to the marriage and the family" (*FC* 22).

E. Marriage and Society

The institution of marriage is essential to society. For the Israelite, the celebration of matrimony was a communal event. In marriage, the command of God to be fruitful and multiply was realized. The union of man and woman, like all things of the world, was recognized as a gift of creation. Entire villages would come together to rejoice and offer thanksgiving for the bond of husband and wife. Marriage was seen as a sacred celebration.

II. Marriage as a Sacrament

A. In the Old Testament, marriage increasingly reflected the covenant shared between God and Israel, marked by love and fidelity. This image is not destroyed in the New Testament.

In the person of Jesus Christ, the relationship of man and woman in matrimony is raised to a new level.

The new "way" proclaimed by the Son of God does not ignore or minimize the true nature of the marriage covenant revealed in the Old Testament. On the contrary, Jesus continually affirms and supports the holiness of matrimony. In his word and example, marriage is held in high esteem. The Wedding Feast of Cana is a prime example.

In the second chapter of John's Gospel, Jesus, Mary and the disciples are numbered among the invited guests of a wedding party. According to the scripture text, "on the third day there was a wedding feast at Cana in Galilee, and the mother of Jesus was there. Jesus and his disciples were also invited to the wedding" (Jn 2:1-2). The wedding feast was not uneventful. A shortage of wine and a mother's request allowed the opportunity for Jesus to perform his first sign. He transformed ordinary water into exceptional wine. A celebration of marriage thus became a manifestation of God's glory. "Jesus did this as the beginning of his signs in Cana in Galilee and so revealed his glory, and his disciples began to believe in him" (Jn 2:11). Cana was both an event of God's glory and an affirmation of the institution of marriage. According to the *Catechism*, "The Church attaches great importance to Jesus' presence at the wedding at Cana. She sees in it the confirmation of the goodness of marriage and the proclamation that thenceforth marriage will be an efficacious sign of Christ's presence" (*Catechism* 1613). Jesus' support of marriage did not end at Cana.

B. Jesus did not come to abolish the institution of marriage. Rather, he demanded that it be restored.

The union of husband and wife must reflect and project the original plan of God. This plan, however, was not clearly present in the commu-

Gene Plaisted, OSC

nity of Israel at the time of Jesus. In the Gospel of Matthew, the Pharisees repeatedly attempt to test the teaching of Jesus. In one case, the test is centered around the question of divorce. They inquire, "is it lawful for a man to divorce his wife for any cause whatever?" (Mt 19:3). For the Pharisees, divorce was a real possibility — the permission for a man to divorce his wife was given in the law of Moses. For Jesus, the contrary is true. "He said in reply, 'Have you not read that from the beginning the Creator "made them male and female" and said, "For this reason a man shall leave his father and mother and be joined to his wife, and the two shall become one flesh"? So they are no longer two, but one flesh. Therefore, what God has joined together, no human being must separate'" (Mt 19:4-6).

Divorce has no place in the original design of God. The law of Moses is not the negation of God's plan. Instead, divorce was seen by Jesus as the result of the hardness of heart — a closed heart and closed mind. In the words of Jesus, "Because of the hardness of your hearts Moses allowed you to divorce your wives, but from the beginning it was not so" (Mt 19:8). For John Paul II, Jesus "reveals the original truth of marriage, the truth of the 'beginning,' and, freeing man from his hardness of heart, he makes man capable of realizing this truth in its entirety" (*FC* 13).

The dynamic inaugurated by the Son of God regarding the holy bond of marriage is summarized in the *Catechism of the Catholic Church*. "In his preaching Jesus unequivocally taught the original meaning of the union of man and woman as the Creator willed it from the beginning. The matrimonial union of man and woman is indissoluble. God himself has determined it: 'what therefore God has joined together, let no man put asunder'" (*Catechism* 1614; cf. Mt 19:6).

Matrimony itself becomes a manifestation of God's grace. As a sign of Christ's loving presence, the institution of marriage is raised to a new level. In the Old Testament, marriage was understood in the context of God's covenant with the people of Israel. In the New Testament, marriage is a sign of the covenant of Christ and his Church. As a living sign of God's grace, the marriage of two baptized persons is a sacrament.

A sacrament is defined as "perceptible signs of Christ (words and actions) accessible to our human nature." Further, "by the action of Christ and the power of the Holy Spirit they make present efficaciously the grace that they signify" (*Catechism* 1084). As one of the seven sacraments, marriage is an authentic symbol of the salvation event. Through the gift of grace, the baptized married couple are able to grow close to each other and God. John Paul II writes: "As a memorial, the sacrament gives them the grace and duty of commemorating the great works of God and of bearing witness to them before their children. As actuation, it gives them the grace and duty of putting into practice in the present, towards each other and their children, the demands of love which forgives and redeems. As prophecy, it gives them the grace and duty of living and bearing witness to the hope of the future encounter with Christ" (*FC* 13).

Prior to Christ, the original plan of God for the institution of marriage was blurred by sin and loss. Original sin ruptured the true communion of man and woman. As stated earlier, Moses allowed for divorce because of the hardness associated with the human heart. In Jesus Christ, however, men and women are invited to live in true communion. "By coming to restore the original order of creation disturbed by sin, he himself gives the strength and grace to live marriage in the new dimension of the Reign of God. It is by following Christ, renouncing themselves, and taking up their crosses that spouses will be able to 'receive' the original meaning of marriage and live it with the help of Christ" (*Catechism* 1615 cf. Mt 19:11). In Christ, the yoke is heavy but the burden is light (*Catechism* 1615).

As a true sacrament, the bond of matrimony is thus fixed in the person of Jesus. In their love for each other, marriage makes real their self-giving in the Lord.

C. *Essential Properties (Canon 1056)*

Being an efficacious sign of God's grace is not without consequence. Marriage is marked by specific properties: unity and indissolubility.

According to the Code of Canon Law, marriage is a "covenant between baptized persons (that) has been raised by Christ the Lord to the dignity of a sacrament" (Canon 1055, par. 1). As a sacrament, this covenant is characterized by two properties. The Code declares: "The essential properties of marriage are unity and indissolubility, which in Christian marriage obtain a special firmness in virtue of the sacrament" (Canon 1056).

In marriage, two persons become one flesh. "They 'are called to grow continually in their communion through day to day fidelity to their marriage promise of total mutual self-giving'" (*Catechism* 1644; cf. *FC* 19). The Fathers of the Second Vatican Council identify "unity" as a distinct quality of Christian marriage. "The unity of marriage, distinctly recognized by our Lord, is made clear in the equal personal dignity which must be accorded to man and wife in mutual and unreserved affection." Furthermore, "outstanding courage is required for the constant fulfillment of the duties of this Christian calling: spouses, therefore will need grace for leading a holy life: they will eagerly practice a love that is firm, generous, and prompt to sacrifice and will ask for it in their prayers" (*GS* 49).

Mutual and unreserved affection is synonymous with a life of true faithfulness. "Love seeks to be definitive: it cannot be an arrangement until further notice. The intimate union of marriage, as a mutual giving of two persons, and the good of children, demand total fidelity from the spouses and require an unbreakable union between them" (*Catechism* 1646; cf. *GS* 48 §1).

The union of husband and wife in the Sacrament of Marriage is also indissoluble. The marriage bond, concluded and consummated, between two baptized persons cannot be dissolved. Reflecting the love of Christ for his Church, the institution of matrimony is a life-long commitment of love. "This bond, which results from the free human act of the spouses and their consummation of the marriage, is a reality, henceforth irrevocable, and gives rise to a covenant guaranteed by God's fidelity" (*Catechism* 1640).

The Sacrament of Marriage cannot be separated from the person of Christ. Jesus Christ is the source and focus of authentic unified and indissoluble marriage. Without destroying the original plan of creation, marriage is fulfilled and elevated in the Son of God. The Christian Sacrament of Marriage is different from the marriage that existed in the Garden of Eden, before the Fall of Man. Christian marriage is always rooted in the person of Jesus Christ.

James L. Shaffer

III. Marriage as a Public Ceremony

A. In the Church

In virtually every culture, society and legal system in the world, there is some type of legal formality which must be observed in order for a marriage to take place. The Catholic Church is no exception. For marriages between two non-Catholic partners, some form of public legal ceremony suffices to constitute marriage. For marriage "in the Church," however, more is required for and from the partners. That is, for marriages in which at least one partner is a Catholic who has not formally loft the Church, it is required that the spouses follow a legal procedure particular to the Church. Such weddings must be simultaneously recognized as legal and valid according to civil law as well. But from the perspective of faith, it is essential that the Catholic party adhere to the requirements of the Church when marrying, in order that he or she may be truly married in God's sight.

B. Exchange of Consent

According to Catholic Theology and Canon Law, "Marriage is brought about through the consent of the parties" (Canon 1057, par. 1). That is to say, the spouses themselves bring about the marriage when they exchange consent, or, in other words, they "mutually give and accept each other" by an act of the will (see Canon 1057).

The question may arise as to why an act so personal and exclusive must take place in accordance with civil and Church regulations. The answer lies in the fact that the covenant of life and love which comes into existence when a man and a woman validly and legally exchange consent affects the larger community, both civil and ecclesial. For the good of the spouses, the marriage bond must be protected and the rights and obligations which accompany it must be clearly understood. Likewise, for any children born of the marriage, there must be legally assured care and protection. Society is built upon the family unit, and both Church and State wisely see fit to regulate and safeguard the institution of marriage from which families come into being in modern times, as they have throughout history.

Families which are not built upon marriage do not have the stability and commitment of the marriage bond upon which to rely in times of hardship, as well as in good times. The exchange of consent signifies a permanent commitment and is essential in the covenant relationship between husband and wife.

C. *According to Canon Law*

When at least one spouse is a Catholic who has not formally left the Church (for example, by joining another religion), the marriage must take place according to the norms set forth in the Church's Code of Canon Law. In other words, the marriage must take place according to the "Canonical Form" prescribed by the Church, or at least with the Church's permission. If Catholics knowingly ignore this requirement, they are not married in the eyes of the Church, and are living in an objective situation which not only goes against Church law, but is also seriously sinful. To marry without the blessing, permission or dispensation of the Church (depending upon the circumstances) is equivalent, in the Church's understanding, to not being married at all. Thus, the so-called "Form" to be followed is extremely important.

A marriage celebrated according to "Form" is one which takes place in the presence of a Catholic bishop, priest or deacon (in ordinary circumstances) who has the authority (or delegation) to witness the exchange of consent, and in the presence of two witnesses. Ordinarily a priest or deacon in the parish boundaries where either party lives will be the person who has the authority to assist at the wedding. Other priests or deacons may be given the authority to witness a marriage, but the parish of either party should be the place to begin the process of marriage preparation. If a Catholic, or both Catholic partners, do not have an affiliation with a parish, they should begin to establish one with the parish of the place where they live.

D. Within the Mass

1. Two Catholics

If two Catholics are to be married, the wedding must take place according to the "Form" spoken of above, preferably within the celebration of the Mass. This is known as a Nuptial Mass. Within the celebration of the Eucharist, the Sacrament of Matrimony and other rituals (like the exchange of rings) take place after the homily. There is also a special Nuptial blessing bestowed upon the newlyweds immediately after the "Our Father."

In bringing together the sacraments of the Eucharist and Matrimony, the Church desires to make clearly evident the connection between Christ's giving himself completely out of love for his Church (often referred to in scripture as his bride), and the self-giving nature of the Sacrament of Matrimony. The true and full meaning of both sacraments is most evident when both spouses are Catholic and are free to receive the Eucharist immediately after exchanging their wedding vows, presuming they are free of serious sin. (It is always recommended that the spouses receive the Sacrament of Reconciliation before the wedding in order to strengthen them and prepare them to receive the Sacrament of Matrimony fruitfully and, if need be to free them of serious sin.)

2. Mixed Marriages

Being united in mind and heart at the ceremony, and sharing a common faith, a Catholic couple is less likely to encounter obstacles to communion of life together, as might occur if there were some significant aspect of life which they did not share from the outset, such as faith.

It is certainly not impossible, and even quite common, that Catholics enter into marriage with non-Catholics — a "mixed marriage." But the couples should be aware that the Church wishes to inform those who are preparing to enter mixed marriages that the absence of sharing the same faith could potentially lead to difficulties in their life together.

The Code of Canon Law refers to a mixed marriage as the marriage between a Catholic and a baptized non-Catholic (e.g., a Baptist, Methodist or Presbyterian). In the understanding of the Church, any marriage which takes place between two baptized persons is a sacrament, and when one of those persons is a Catholic, the marriage must take place under the auspices of the Catholic Church. It is encouraged that mixed marriages take place within the celebration of the Mass, but for good reasons, they may take place outside of Mass. In fact, mixed marriages need not necessarily take place in a Catholic ceremony. With proper permission, and a "dispensation from Form," the wedding of a Catholic and a baptized non-Catholic may take place in the church of the non-Catholic party. The reasons for such allowances are to accommodate the party whose faith might be stronger, or to make it possible that a non-Catholic minister who is a relative or friend of the non-Catholic may perform the ceremony. It may also be the case that the family of the non-Catholic party would have difficulties attending a Catholic ceremony. Thus, the Church does not insist on a wedding in a Catholic church, but the preference is always that the vows be exchanged in a Catholic ceremony. The priest or deacon who performs the wedding (or is consulted by the couple) can be helpful in further explaining the circumstances that would lend themselves to making the decision to marry in a place and ceremony other than a Catholic church.

E. Outside the Mass: Marriage between a Catholic and a Non-Baptized Person.

Unlike marriages that take place between two baptized persons, the marriage between a Catholic and a non-baptized person (e.g., someone of Jewish, Moslem or Buddhist faith) is not a sacrament. Nonetheless, a natural bond of marriage comes into being when one or both parties is non-baptized. In other words, a true marriage may exist, even though it does not enjoy the special firmness of a sacramental marriage. Since the reception of the sacrament would require the sacramental giving and receiving of love, this is not possible when one of the partners does not participate in the sacrament because he or she has not received the primary sacrament of Baptism. However, the Church permits and presides over such natural bonds of marriage when a Catholic is involved, provided there are no other impediments to marriage, nor obstacles to faith. Even though the Sacrament of Matrimony is not celebrated, the natural bond of marriage is witnessed by the Church's minister and a blessing of the couple is imparted, invoking God's help and protection.

It is the Church's practice that such a wedding ceremony not take place within the celebration of the Mass, to stress the fact that the marriage itself is not a sacrament, and so as not to offend or confuse those non-baptized persons who are present, including one of the spouses. It should be well noted that such weddings must be recognized by the Church in order for the Catholic party to be validly married.

Unlike weddings between a Catholic and a baptized non-Catholic (mixed marriages), which require the permission of the Catholic party's bishop, the wedding between a Catholic and a non-baptized person requires a special dispensation in order to be valid, and another dispensation is necessary if the wedding is to take place without observance of the canonical Form. That is to say, if such a wedding is not to take place in the presence of a properly authorized bishop, priest or deacon, a dispensation (not merely a permission) is absolutely necessary. The priest of the parish of the Catholic party will best be able to further explain the details of such a wedding, but it will suffice to say here that the Church takes special measures to point out to a Catholic who wishes to marry a non-baptized person that there are important considerations to be weighed in making such a decision.

Faith is far too important a dimension of life to be ignored when making the decision to marry, and the Church, with her legal requirements, wishes to be certain that Catholics realize the complexities involved in marriage to a non-baptized person, and the difficulties such a marriage might present to the Catholic and the non-Catholic alike (such as being able to continue practicing the Catholic faith, and raising as Catholics any children born of the marriage). So essential is the Church's role in safeguarding the faith of the Catholic party that without both the permission and dispensation on the part of the competent Church authority for such a marriage to take place, the marriage would be invalid, or to use another phrase, null and void. This permission or

James L. Shaffer

dispensation presupposes that both parties know and do not exclude the essential ends or properties of marriage and the obligations assumed by the Catholic party concerning the baptism and education of children in the Catholic Church (*Catechism* 1635; see Code of Canon Law, c. 1125). For a Catholic to knowingly ignore his or her obligation to have the marriage recognized by the Church would mean that the wedding does not occur "in God's eyes," and culpability of grave sin is involved.

All Catholics should realize that the Church must somehow be involved both in preparation for and celebration of marriages, even if only one party is Catholic and the couple plans on marrying in a place other than a Catholic church or chapel. It is best to consult a Catholic priest or deacon at the beginning of any process of preparation to marry.

IV. Marriage as a Total Commitment of Self

A. Heart, Mind and Body

"Conjugal love involves a totality, in which all the elements of the person enter — appeal of the body and instinct, power of feeling and affectivity, aspiration of the spirit and of will. It aims at a deeply personal unity, a unity that, beyond union in one flesh, leads to forming one heart and soul; it demands *indissolubility* and *faithfulness* in definitive mutual giving, and it is open to *fertility*" (*FC* 13).

With these words, the *Catechism* (1643) speaks about the depth of the union between husband and wife. Far more than simply involving one aspect, or several aspects, of the lives of the two individuals, marriage involves a total giving of oneself to another. Indeed, due to the marriage vows, married people share every dimension of life together. While they remain individuals before God, they are, as a result of marriage and especially the Sacrament of Matrimony, more closely united to another human being than would ever be possible. There exist many types of human relationships in this world (for example, parent-child, siblings, friends and relatives), but marriage is graced by a special sacrament signifying the most intimate relationship human beings can have, after that with God himself.

The union of husband and wife is first a union of heart and will. Thus, love between a man and woman must first exist and be confirmed in the public vows of marriage before it can be lived as a total communion of persons. Once a marriage has been celebrated, that is, once the marriage ceremony has taken place, married life begins. Only in marriage can such love be expressed fully in a life lived together, always considering the other as important as oneself. Spouses "are called to grow continually in their communion through day-to-day fidelity to their marriage promise of total mutual self-giving" (FC 19).

B. Sexual Union

The sexual union of a husband and wife is a manifestation of true love. "Have you not read that at the beginning, the Creator 'made them male and female' and said, 'For this reason, a man shall leave his father and mother and be joined to his wife, and the two shall become one flesh'? So they are no longer two, but one flesh" (Mt 19:4-6). Just as marriage itself is ordered toward the good of the spouses and the procreation and education of children, so too is married love (see Catechism 1652; see also Canon 1055).

1. For the Good of the Spouses

The Second Vatican Council taught, "Authentic married love is caught up into divine love and is directed and enriched by the redemptive power of Christ and the salvific action of the Church, with the result that the spouses are effectively led to God. . . Thus, they increasingly further their own perfection and their mutual sanctification, and together they render glory to God" (GS 48).

Since sexual union is an aspect of married love, it was intended by God to be at the service of the good of the spouses. This "good" of the spouses comprises every aspect of life, serving to strengthen them and help them to grow in every way, especially spiritually. In the plan of the Creator, sexual union of married persons was meant to be a means of deepening the bond that unites two people. Sexual union of husband and wife must at least be a possibility in order for a true marriage to take place. This union was intended by God to be pleasurable, but conjugal love goes beyond physical pleasure. It is considered the highest expression of love because it involves, or should involve, every dimension of the two persons: emotional, mental, spiritual and physical union. Thus, this purpose of married sexuality is often referred to as "unitive."

It is only within marriage that sexual union takes on the meaning that God willed it to have. In the Church's moral teaching, it is asserted that there is a false giving of self when sexual union occurs outside of the marriage covenant. Furthermore, true self giving and oneness are meant to be permanent, for in Jesus' own words, "what God has joined together, no human being must separate" (Mt 19:6).

2. Procreation

The other end or purpose of marriage, as well as of married love expressed in sexual union, is the procreation and education of children. That is to say, marriage and married love is not simply something willed or intended by God for the spouses themselves, but rather such love is also directed towards others. Each and every marriage must be open to the procreation of new life. The word "procreation," and not "creation," is used in order to highlight the fact that the couple cooperates with God the Creator in bringing about new life. Since it is God himself who created man and woman, established the institution of marriage, and calls husband and wife to "be fertile and multiply" (Gn 1:28), the Church reminds those who are united in marriage, and especially the Sacrament of Matrimony, that married love goes beyond the individual, and even beyond the couple, and is ordered to an openness to others. In God's plan, most married couples are called to bring forth new life as a result of their marital union, but all couples are called to be open to accepting children according to the will of God. The desire to do God's will is itself a form of praise and service to God.

In the Church's constant understanding, just as every marriage must be ordered to the good of the spouses and the procreation of children, so too must every act of sexual union in married life. Sexual union goes against the marriage bond if it is not a genuine expression of conjugal love, or if it is not open to potential new life.

Naturally, the Church does not believe that children can or should be conceived each and every time a husband and wife express their love in sexual union, but neither should they make conception absolutely impossible. Couples have the right and the responsibility to decide how many children they feel they can bear and raise within their means and capabilities, but in the end, the number of children they have or will not have depends upon God. Spouses are called to respect his will and the order of nature that he established. Husbands and wives can employ natural means in assisting in procreation or avoiding conception, but should never strive to exclude the will and work of God in bringing about new life. Through Natural Family Planning married couples are able to lovingly exercise responsible procreation.

a. Natural Family Planning

Natural Family Planning (NFP) is the natural means that is approved by the Church for spacing births or avoiding conception indefinitely with good reason.

In his encyclical, *The Gospel of Life*, John Paul II writes, "In its true meaning, responsible procreation requires couples to be obedient to the Lord's call and to act as faithful interpreters of his plan. This happens when the family is generously open to new lives, and when couples maintain an attitude of openness and service to life, even if, for serious reasons and in respect for the moral law, they choose to avoid a new birth for the time being or indefinitely. The moral law obliges them in every case to control the impulse of instinct and passion, and to respect the biological laws inscribed in their person. It is precisely this respect which makes legitimate, at the service of responsible procreation, the use of natural methods of regulating fertility" (*EV* 97).

Natural Family Planning (NFP) methods have improved over time due to an increased scientific understanding of reproductive biology, so that the so-called "Rhythm Method" is outdated. The NFP method takes into consideration the important physical signs of fertility and the possibility of conception, and is highly effective if used properly. Regu-

Gene Plaisted, OSC

lar attention to the method is absolutely essential to its success, and the cooperation of husband and wife is necessary. This spirit of collaboration greatly strengthens and deepens the marital relationship. Together with the loving sacrifice and effort required, it is part of the reason that the Church considers the method to be morally acceptable. In order to learn more about the method, contact your local parish for information about classes that are made available by the Church to assist couples in this important aspect of married life.

b. Some Recent Issues Regarding Conception

Just as the Church teaches that artificial means of contraception go against the plan of the Creator by frustrating nature's way by using unnatural methods, so too does the Church disapprove of artificial means of conceiving children. Obviously, there is a difference in mentality between artificial conception and artificial contraception, the first being a means of bringing about new life, the second being a means of avoiding new life. Yet in both processes, the two aspects of marital sexuality are separated beyond the intention of God the Creator. In using artificial contraception (e.g., condoms, diaphragm; also I.U.D.'s and birth control pills which do and can have abortifacient effects), the good of the spouse (or the unitive aspect) is stressed to the exclusion of the procreative aspect of sexual union. With artificial conception (e.g., artificial insemination), the opposite is true, and there is the exclusion of one aspect of sexual intercourse (the unitive aspect) in favor of procreation. In God's plan, the two aspects of married love were meant to be united in every act, and the Church declares that this intention must be respected. There are other problems with the various methods of artificial conception as they exist today, for example, that fertilized eggs (i.e., new individual human lives) are often discarded. In reality, the dignity of life and of procreation are not respected.

c. Other Concerns

Much more could be written with regard to married love and human sexuality, but this work is meant to be a brief presentation of Church teaching. The Church's understanding that pre-marital sexual relations, adultery, homosexual acts and masturbation are immoral actions must also be taken into account when speaking of human sexuality. Oftentimes, engaged couples wonder (and even agonize) as to "how far they can go" with regard to intimate contact, before compromising their moral integrity. The rule is that genital sexual intercourse (that is, sexual orgasm when the genitals of a male and a female are joined) is always reserved for marriage. Any other act that leads to orgasm is against the moral law. The Church realizes that there is a certain amount of difficulty in controlling sexual impulses, especially when two people are engaged to be married. However, certain actions are reserved for married couples and are morally wrong outside marital life.

Likewise, even married couples must remember that sexual intercourse must always be at the service of life and love, so that sexual sins are possible if intercourse is not an expression of conjugal love (e.g., if it is imposed upon a spouse without his or her full consent), or if orgasm occurs in such a way that it is absolutely impossible that conception could ever take place (e.g., an act of oral sex that leads to orgasm).

Engaged and married couples must continually strive, with the help of grace, to follow the laws of nature and of God in living out their sexuality. Despite the difficulties experienced by some, the Church constantly calls our attention to the grace of God, the gift of forgiveness and the power of true love in living the Christian way of life. "With God all things are possible" (Mt 19:26).

Gene Plaisted, OSC

Rite of Entrance

Opening Prayers

Selection OP-1

Priest: Father,
you have made the bond of marriage
a holy mystery,
a symbol of Christ's love for his Church.
Hear our prayers for N. and N.
With faith in you and in each other
they pledge their love today.
May their lives always bear witness
to the reality of that love.
We ask you this
through our Lord Jesus Christ, your Son,
who lives and reigns with you and the Holy Spirit,
one God, for ever and ever.

Response: Amen.

Selection OP-2

Priest: Father,
hear our prayers for N. and N.,
who today are united in marriage before your altar.
Give them your blessing,
and strengthen their love for each other.
We ask you this
through our Lord Jesus Christ, your Son,
who lives and reigns with you and the Holy Spirit,
one God, for ever and ever.

Response: Amen.

<u>Selection OP-3</u>

Priest: Almighty God,
hear our prayers for N. and N.,
who have come here today
to be united in the sacrament of marriage.
Increase their faith in you and in each other,
and through them bless your Church
[with Christian children].
We ask you this
through our Lord Jesus Christ, your Son,
who lives and reigns with you and the Holy Spirit,
one God, for ever and ever.

Response: Amen.

<u>Selection OP-4</u>

Priest: Father,
when you created mankind,
you willed that man and wife should be one.
Bind N. and N.
in the loving union of marriage,
and make their love fruitful
so that they may be living witnesses
to your divine love in the world.
We ask you this
through our Lord Jesus Christ, your Son,
who lives and reigns with you and the Holy Spirit,
one God, for ever and ever.

Response: Amen.

Liturgy of the Word

Old Testament Readings

Selection OT-1 (Genesis 1:26-28, 31a)

A reading from the Book of Genesis.

Then God said:
"Let us make man in our image, after our likeness.
Let them have dominion over the fish of the sea,
    the birds of the air, and the cattle,
    and over all the wild animals
    and all the creatures that crawl on the ground."
God created man in his image;
    in the image of God he created him;
    male and female he created them.
God blessed them, saying:
    "Be fertile and multiply;
    fill the earth and subdue it.
Have dominion over the fish of the sea, the birds of the air,
    and all the living things that move on the earth."
God looked at everything he had made, and he found it very good.

The word of the Lord.   **Response:** *Thanks be to God.*

Selection OT-2 (Genesis 2:18-24)

A reading from the Book of Genesis.

The Lord God said: "It is not good for the man to be alone.
I will make a suitable partner for him."
So the Lord God formed out of the ground
    various wild animals and various birds of the air,
    and he brought them to the man to see what he would call
       them;

whatever the man called each of them would be its name.
The man gave names to all the cattle,
    all the birds of the air, and all wild animals;
    but none proved to be the suitable partner for the man.

So the Lord God cast a deep sleep on the man,
    and while he was asleep,
    he took out one of his ribs and closed up its place with flesh.
The Lord God then built up into a woman the rib
    that he had taken from the man.
When he brought her to the man, the man said:

    "This one, at last, is bone of my bones
      and flesh of my flesh;
    This one shall be called 'woman,'
      for out of 'her man' this one has been taken."

That is why a man leaves his father and mother
    and clings to his wife,
    and the two of them become one body.

The word of the Lord.   **Response:** *Thanks be to God.*

Selection OT-3 (Genesis 24:48-51, 58-67)

A reading from the Book of Genesis.

The servant of Abraham said to Laban:
"I bowed down in worship to the Lord,
    blessing the Lord, the God of my master Abraham,
    who had led me on the right road
    to obtain the daughter of my master's kinsman for his son.
If, therefore, you have in mind to show true loyalty to my master,
    let me know;
    but if not, let me know that, too.
I can then proceed accordingly."

Laban and his household said in reply:
    "This thing comes from the Lord;
    we can say nothing to you either for or against it.
Here is Rebekah, ready for you;
    take her with you,

that she may become the wife of your master's son,
as the LORD has said."

So they called Rebekah and asked her,
"Do you wish to go with this man?"
She answered, "I do."
At this they allowed their sister Rebekah and her nurse to take leave,
along with Abraham's servant and his men.
Invoking a blessing on Rebekah, they said:

"Sister, may you grow
into thousands of myriads;
And may your descendants gain possession
of the gates of their enemies!"

Then Rebekah and her maids started out;
they mounted their camels and followed the man.
So the servant took Rebekah and went on his way.

Meanwhile Isaac had gone from Beer-lahai-roi
and was living in the region of the Negeb.
One day toward evening he went out . . . in the field,
and as he looked around, he noticed that camels were
approaching.
Rebekah, too, was looking about, and when she saw him,
she alighted from her camel and asked the servant,
"Who is the man out there, walking through the fields toward us?"
"That is my master," replied the servant.
Then she covered herself with her veil.

The servant recounted to Isaac all the things he had done.
Then Isaac took Rebekah into his tent;
he married her, and thus she became his wife.
In his love for her Isaac found solace
after the death of his mother Sarah.

The word of the Lord. **Response:** *Thanks be to God.*

Selection OT-4 (Tobit 7:6-14)

A reading from the Book of Tobit.

Raphael and Tobiah entered the house of Raguel and greeted him.
Raguel sprang up and kissed Tobiah, shedding tears of joy.
But when he heard that Tobit had lost his eyesight,
 he was grieved and wept aloud.
He said to Tobiah:
 "My child, God bless you!
You are the son of a noble and good father.
But what a terrible misfortune
 that such a righteous and charitable man
 should be afflicted with blindness!"
He continued to weep in the arms of his kinsman Tobiah.
His wife Edna also wept for Tobit;
 and even their daughter Sarah began to weep.

Afterward, Raguel slaughtered a ram from the flock
 and gave them a cordial reception.
When they had bathed and reclined to eat,
 Tobiah said to Raphael, "Brother Azariah,
 ask Raguel to let me marry my kinswoman Sarah."
Raguel overheard the words;
 so he said to the boy:
 "Eat and drink and be merry tonight,
 for no man is more entitled to marry my daughter Sarah
 than you, brother.
Besides, not even I have the right to give her to anyone but you,
 because you are my closest relative.
But I will explain the situation to you very frankly.
I have given her in marriage to seven men,
 all of whom were kinsmen of ours,
 and all died on the very night they approached her.
But now, son, eat and drink.
I am sure the Lord will look after you both."
Tobiah answered, "I will eat or drink nothing
 until you set aside what belongs to me."
Raguel said to him: "I will do it.
She is yours according to the decree of the Book of Moses.

Your marriage to her has been decided in heaven!
Take your kinswoman
>from now on you are her love,
>and she is your beloved.
She is yours today and ever after.
And tonight, son, may the Lord of heaven prosper you both.
May he grant you mercy and peace."
Then Raguel called his daughter Sarah, and she came to him.
He took her by the hand and gave her to Tobiah with the words:
>"Take her according to the law.
According to the decree written in the Book of Moses she is your wife.
Take her and bring her back safely to your father.
And may the God of heaven grant both of you peace and prosperity."
He then called her mother and told her to bring a scroll,
>so that he might draw up a marriage contract
>stating that he gave Sarah to Tobiah as his wife
>according to the decree of the Mosaic law.
Her mother brought the scroll,
>and he drew up the contract,
>to which they affixed their seals.
Afterward they began to eat and drink.

The word of the Lord.   **Response:** *Thanks be to God.*

Selection OT-5 (Tobit 8:4b-8)

A reading from the Book of Tobit.

On their wedding night Tobiah arose from bed and said to his wife,
>"Sister, get up. Let us pray and beg our Lord
>to have mercy on us and to grant us deliverance."
Sarah got up, and they started to pray
>and beg that deliverance might be theirs.
They began with these words:

>"Blessed are you, O God of our fathers;
>>praised be your name forever and ever.
>Let the heavens and all your creation
>>praise you forever.

You made Adam and you gave him his wife Eve
    to be his help and support;
    and from these two the human race descended.
You said, 'It is not good for the man to be alone;
    let us make him a partner like himself.'
Now, Lord, you know that I take this wife of mine
    not because of lust,
    but for a noble purpose.
Call down your mercy on me and on her,
    and allow us to live together to a happy old age."

They said together, "Amen, amen."

The word of the Lord.　　　　　　　　　**Response:** *Thanks be to God.*

Selection OT-6 (Proverbs 31:10-13, 19-20, 30-31)

A reading from the Book of Proverbs.

When one finds a worthy wife,
    her value is far beyond pearls.
Her husband, entrusting his heart to her,
    has an unfailing prize.
She brings him good, and not evil,
    all the days of her life.
She obtains wool and flax
    and makes cloth with skillful hands.
She puts her hands to the distaff,
    and her fingers ply the spindle.
She reaches out her hands to the poor,
    and extends her arms to the needy.
Charm is deceptive and beauty fleeting;
    the woman who fears the LORD is to be praised.
Give her a reward of her labors,
    and let her works praise her at the city gates.

The word of the Lord.　　　　　　　　　**Response:** *Thanks be to God.*

Selection OT-7 (Song of Songs 2:8-10, 14, 16a; 8:6-7a)

A reading from the Song of Songs.

Hark! my lover – here he comes
> springing across the mountains,
> leaping across the hills.
My lover is like a gazelle
> or a young stag.
Here he stands behind our wall,
> gazing through the windows,
> peering through the lattices.
My lover speaks; he says to me,
> "Arise, my beloved, my dove, my beautiful one, and come!

"O my dove in the clefts of the rock,
> in the secret recesses of the cliff,
Let me see you,
> let me hear your voice,
For your voice is sweet,
> and you are lovely."

My lover belongs to me and I to him.
> He says to me:

"Set me as a seal on your heart,
> as a seal on your arm;
For stern as death is love,
> relentless as the nether-world is devotion;
> its flames are a blazing fire.
Deep waters cannot quench love,
> nor floods sweep it away."

The word of the Lord.   **Response:** *Thanks be to God.*

Selection OT-8 (Sirach 26:1-4; 13-16)

A reading from the Book of Sirach.

Blessed the husband of a good wife,
> twice-lengthened are his days;

A worthy wife brings joy to her husband,
    peaceful and full is his life.
A good wife is a generous gift
    bestowed upon him who fears the LORD;
Be he rich or poor, his heart is content,
    and a smile is ever on his face.

A gracious wife delights her husband,
    her thoughtfulness puts flesh on his bones;
A gift from the LORD is her governed speech,
    and her firm virtue is of surpassing worth.
Choicest of blessings is a modest wife,
    priceless her chaste soul.
A holy and decent woman adds grace upon grace;
    indeed, no price is worthy of her temperate soul.
Like the sun rising in the LORD's heavens,
    the beauty of a virtuous wife is the radiance of her home.

The word of the Lord.   **Response:** *Thanks be to God.*

Selection OT-9 (Jeremiah 31:31-32a. 33-34a)

A reading from the Book of the Prophet Jeremiah.

The days are coming, says the LORD,
    when I will make a new covenant with the house of Israel
    and the house of Judah.
It will not be like the covenant I made with their fathers:
    the day I took them by the hand
    to lead them forth from the land of Egypt
But this is the covenant which I will make
    with the house of Israel after those days, says the LORD.
I will place my law within them, and write it upon their hearts;
    I will be their God, and they shall be my people.
No longer will they have need to teach their friends and relatives
    how to know the LORD.
All, from least to greatest, shall know me, says the LORD.

The word of the Lord.   **Response:** *Thanks be to God.*

Responsorial Psalms

Selection RP-1 (Psalm 33:12 and 18, 20-21, 22)

Response: *The earth is full of the goodness of the Lord.*

> Blessed the nation whose God is the LORD,
>> the people he has chosen for his own inheritance.
> But see, the eyes of the LORD are upon those who fear him,
>> upon those who hope for his kindness.

Response: *The earth is full of the goodness of the Lord.*

> Our soul waits for the LORD,
>> who is our help and our shield,
> For in him our hearts rejoice;
>> in his holy name we trust.

Response: *The earth is full of the goodness of the Lord.*

> May your kindness, O LORD, be upon us
>> who have put our hope in you.

Response: *The earth is full of the goodness of the Lord.*

Selection RP-2 (Psalm 34:2-3, 4-5, 6-7, 8-9)

Response: *I will bless the Lord at all times.*
or: *Taste and see the goodness of the Lord.*

> I will bless the LORD at all times;
>> his praise shall be ever in my mouth.
> Let my soul glory in the LORD;
>> the lowly will hear me and be glad.

Response: *I will bless the Lord at all times.*
or: *Taste and see the goodness of the Lord.*

> Glorify the LORD with me,
>> let us together extol his name.
> I sought the LORD, and he answered me
>> and delivered me from all my fears.

Response: *I will bless the Lord at all times.*
or: *Taste and see the goodness of the Lord.*

Look to him that you may be radiant with joy,
and your faces may not blush with shame.
When the poor one called out, the LORD heard,
and from all his distress he saved him.

Response: *I will bless the Lord at all times.*
or: *Taste and see the goodness of the Lord.*

The angel of the LORD encamps
around those who fear him, and delivers them.
Taste and see how good the LORD is;
blessed the man who takes refuge in him.

Response: *I will bless the Lord at all times.*
or: *Taste and see the goodness of the Lord.*

Selection RP-3 (Psalm 103:1-2, 8 and 13, 17-18a)

Response: *The Lord is kind and merciful.*
or: *The Lord's kindness is everlasting to those who fear him.*

Bless the LORD, O my soul;
and all my being, bless his holy name.
Bless the LORD, O my soul,
and forget not all his benefits.

Response: *The Lord is kind and merciful.*
or: *The Lord's kindness is everlasting to those who fear him.*

Merciful and gracious is the LORD,
slow to anger and abounding in kindness.
As a father has compassion on his children,
so the LORD has compassion on those who fear him.

Response: *The Lord is kind and merciful.*
or: *The Lord's kindness is everlasting to those who fear him.*

But the kindness of the LORD is from eternity
to eternity toward those who fear him,
And his justice towards children's children
among those who keep his covenant.

Response: *The Lord is kind and merciful.*
or: *The Lord's kindness is everlasting to those who fear him.*

Selection RP-4 (Psalm 112:1bc-2, 3-4, 5-7a, 7b-8, 9)

Response: *Blessed the man who greatly delights in the Lord's commands.*
or: *Alleluia.*

Blessed the man who fears the LORD,
    who greatly delights in his commands.
His posterity shall be mighty upon the earth;
    the upright generation shall be blessed.

Response: *Blessed the man who greatly delights in the Lord's commands.*
or: *Alleluia.*

Wealth and riches shall be in his house;
    his generosity shall endure forever.
Light shines through the darkness for the upright;
    he is gracious and merciful and just.

Response: *Blessed the man who greatly delights in the Lord's commands.*
or: *Alleluia.*

Well for the man who is gracious and lends,
    who conducts his affairs with justice;
He shall never be moved;
    the just one shall be in everlasting remembrance.
An evil report he shall not fear.

Response: *Blessed the man who greatly delights in the Lord's commands.*
or: *Alleluia.*

His heart is firm, trusting in the LORD.
His heart is steadfast; he shall not fear
    till he looks down upon his foes.

Response: *Blessed the man who greatly delights in the Lord's commands.*
or: *Alleluia.*

Lavishly he gives to the poor;
    his generosity shall endure forever;
    his horn shall be exalted in glory.

Response: *Blessed the man who greatly delights in the Lord's commands.*
or: *Alleluia.*

Gene Plaisted, OSC

Selection RP-5 (Psalm 128:1-2, 3, 4-5)

Response: *Blessed are those who fear the Lord.*
or: *See how the Lord blesses those who fear him.*
           Blessed are you who fear the LORD,
              who walk in his ways!
           For you shall eat the fruit of your handiwork;
              blessed shall you be, and favored.
Response: *Blessed are those who fear the Lord.*
or: *See how the Lord blesses those who fear him.*
           Your wife shall be like a fruitful vine
              in the recesses of your home;
           Your children like olive plants
              around your table
Response: *Blessed are those who fear the Lord.*
or: *See how the Lord blesses those who fear him.*
           Behold, thus is the man blessed
              who fears the LORD.
           The LORD bless you from Zion:
              may you see the prosperity of Jerusalem
              all the days of your life.
Response: *Blessed are those who fear the Lord.*
or: *See how the Lord blesses those who fear him.*

Selection RP-6 (Psalm 145:8-9, 10 and 15, 17-18)

Response: *The Lord is compassionate toward all his works.*
           The LORD is gracious and merciful,
              slow to anger and of great kindness.
           The LORD is good to all
              and compassionate toward all his works.
Response: *The Lord is compassionate toward all his works.*
           Let all your works give you thanks, O LORD,
              and let your faithful ones bless you.
           The eyes of all look hopefully to you
              and you give them their food in due season.
Response: *The Lord is compassionate toward all his works.*
           The LORD is just in all his ways
              and holy in all his works.

The LORD is near to all who call upon him,
   to all who call upon him in truth.
Response: *The Lord is compassionate toward all his works.*

Selection RP-7 (Psalm 148:1-2, 3-4, 9-10, 11-13a, 13c-14a)

Response: *Let all praise the name of the Lord.*
or: *Alleluia.*
   Alleluia.
   Praise the LORD from the heavens,
      praise him in the heights;
   Praise him, all you his angels,
      praise him, all you his hosts.
Response: *Let all praise the name of the Lord.*
or: *Alleluia.*
   Praise him, sun and moon;
      praise him, all you shining stars.
   Praise him, you highest heavens,
      and you waters above the heavens.
Response: *Let all praise the name of the Lord.*
or: *Alleluia.*
   You mountains and all you hills,
      you fruit trees and all you cedars;
   You wild beasts and all tame animals,
      you creeping things and winged fowl.
Response: *Let all praise the name of the Lord.*
or: *Alleluia.*
   Let the kings of the earth and all peoples,
      the princes and all the judges of the earth,
   Young men too, and maidens,
      old men and boys,
   Praise the name of the LORD,
      for his name alone is exalted.
Response: *Let all praise the name of the Lord.*
or: *Alleluia.*
   His majesty is above earth and heaven,
      and he has lifted his horn above the people.
Response: *Let all praise the name of the Lord.*
or: *Alleluia.*

New Testament Readings

Selection NT-1 (Romans 8:31b-35, 37-39)

A reading from the Letter of Saint Paul to the Romans.

Brothers and sisters:
If God is for us, who can be against us?
He did not spare his own Son
    but handed him over for us all,
    will he not also give us everything else along with him?
Who will bring a charge against God's chosen ones?
It is God who acquits us.
Who will condemn?
It is Christ Jesus who died, rather, was raised,
    who also is at the right hand of God,
    who indeed intercedes for us.
What will separate us from the love of Christ?
Will anguish, or distress, or persecution, or famine,
    or nakedness, or peril, or the sword?

No, in all these things, we conquer overwhelmingly
    through him who loved us.
For I am convinced that neither death, nor life,
    nor angels, nor principalities,
    nor present things, nor future things,
    nor powers, nor height, nor depth,
    nor any other creature will be able to separate us
    from the love of God in Christ Jesus our Lord.

The word of the Lord.   **Response:** *Thanks be to God.*

Selection NT-2 — Long Form (Romans 12:1-2, 9-18)

A reading from the Letter of Saint Paul to the Romans.

I urge you, brothers and sisters, by the mercies of God,
    to offer your bodies as a living sacrifice,
    holy and pleasing to God, your spiritual worship.

Do not conform yourselves to this age
    but be transformed by the renewal of your mind,
    that you may discern what is the will of God,
    what is good and pleasing and perfect.

Let love be sincere;
    hate what is evil,
    hold on to what is good;
    love one another with mutual affection;
    anticipate one another in showing honor.
Do not grow slack in zeal,
    be fervent in spirit,
    serve the Lord.
Rejoice in hope,
    endure in affliction,
    persevere in prayer.
Contribute to the needs of the holy ones,
    exercise hospitality.
Bless those who persecute you,
    bless and do not curse them.
Rejoice with those who rejoice,
    weep with those who weep.
Have the same regard for one another;
    do not be haughty but associate with the lowly;
    do not be wise in your own estimation.
Do not repay anyone evil for evil;
    be concerned for what is noble in the sight of all.
If possible, on your part, live at peace with all.

The word of the Lord.   **Response:** *Thanks be to God.*

Selection NT-2 — Short Form (Romans 12:1-2, 9-13)

A reading from the Letter of Saint Paul to the Romans.

I urge you, brothers and sisters, by the mercies of God,
    to offer your bodies as a living sacrifice,
    holy and pleasing to God, your spiritual worship.
Do not conform yourselves to this age
    but be transformed by the renewal of your mind,

that you may discern what is the will of God,
what is good and pleasing and perfect.

Let love be sincere;
hate what is evil,
hold on to what is good;
love one another with mutual affection;
anticipate one another in showing honor.
Do not grow slack in zeal,
be fervent in spirit,
serve the Lord.
Rejoice in hope,
endure in affliction,
persevere in prayer.
Contribute to the needs of the holy ones,
exercise hospitality.

The word of the Lord.   **Response:** *Thanks be to God.*

Selection NT-3 (Romans 15:1b-3a, 5-7, 13)

A reading from the Letter of Saint Paul to the Romans.

Brothers and sisters:
We ought to put up with the failings of the weak and not to please
ourselves;
let each of us please our neighbor for the good,
for building up.
For Christ did not please himself.
May the God of endurance and encouragement
grant you to think in harmony with one another,
in keeping with Christ Jesus,
that with one accord you may with one voice
glorify the God and Father of our Lord Jesus Christ.

Welcome one another, then, as Christ welcomed you,
for the glory of God.
May the God of hope fill you with all joy and peace in believing,
so that you may abound in hope by the power of the Holy Spirit.

The word of the Lord.   **Response:** *Thanks be to God.*

James L. Shaffer

Selection NT-4 (1 Corinthians 6:13c-15a, 17-20)

A reading from the first Letter of Saint Paul to the Corinthians.

Brothers and sisters:
The body is not for immorality, but for the Lord,
    and the Lord is for the body;
    God raised the Lord and will also raise us by his power.

Do you not know that your bodies are members of Christ?
Whoever is joined to the Lord becomes one spirit with him.
Avoid immorality.
Every other sin a person commits is outside the body,
    but the immoral person sins against his own body.
Do you not know that your body
    is a temple of the Holy Spirit within you,
    whom you have from God, and that you are not your own?
For you have been purchased at a price.
Therefore glorify God in your body.

The word of the Lord.   **Response:** *Thanks be to God.*

Selection NT-5 (1 Corinthians 12:31-13:8a)

A reading from the first Letter of Saint Paul to the Corinthians.

Brothers and sisters:
Strive eagerly for the greatest spiritual gifts.

But I shall show you a still more excellent way.

If I speak in human and angelic tongues
    but do not have love,
    I am a resounding gong or a clashing cymbal.
And if I have the gift of prophecy
    and comprehend all mysteries and all knowledge;
    if I have all faith so as to move mountains,
    but do not have love, I am nothing.
If I give away everything I own,
    and if I hand my body over so that I may boast
    but do not have love, I gain nothing.

Love is patient, love is kind.

It is not jealous, is not pompous,
> it is not inflated, it is not rude,
> it does not seek its own interests,
> it is not quick-tempered, it does not brood over injury, it does
>> not rejoice over wrongdoing
> but rejoices with the truth.
It bears all things, believes all things,
> hopes all things, endures all things.

Love never fails.

The word of the Lord.   **Response:** *Thanks be to God.*

Selection NT-6 — Long Form (Ephesians 5:2a, 21-33)

A reading from the Letter of Saint Paul to the Ephesians.

Brothers and sisters:
Live in love, as Christ loved us
> and handed himself over for us.

Be subordinate to one another out of reverence for Christ.
Wives should be subordinate to their husbands as to the Lord.
For the husband is head of his wife
> just as Christ is head of the Church,
> he himself the savior of the body.
As the Church is subordinate to Christ,
> so wives should be subordinate to their husbands in
>> everything.
Husbands, love your wives,
> even as Christ loved the Church
> and handed himself over for her to sanctify her,
> cleansing her by the bath of water with the word,
> that he might present to himself the Church in splendor,
> without spot or wrinkle or any such thing,
> that she might be holy and without blemish.
So also husbands should love their wives as their own bodies.
He who loves his wife loves himself.
For no one hates his own flesh
> but rather nourishes and cherishes it,
> even as Christ does the Church,
> because we are members of his Body.

For this reason a man shall leave his father and his mother
    and be joined to his wife,
and the two shall become one flesh.

This is a great mystery,
    but I speak in reference to Christ and the Church.
In any case, each one of you should love his wife as himself,
    and the wife should respect her husband.

The word of the Lord.   **Response:** *Thanks be to God.*

<u>Selection NT-6 — Short Form (Ephesians 5:2a, 25-32)</u>

A reading from the Letter of Saint Paul to the Ephesians.

Brothers and sisters:
Live in love, as Christ loved us
    and handed himself over for us.

Husbands, love your wives,
        even as Christ loved the Church
        and handed himself over for her to sanctify her,
        cleansing her by the bath of water with the word,
        that he might present to himself the Church in splendor,
        without spot or wrinkle or any such thing,
        that she might be holy and without blemish.
So also husbands should love their wives as their own bodies.
He who loves his wife loves himself.
For no one hates his own flesh
        but rather nourishes and cherishes it,
        even as Christ does the Church,
        because we are members of his Body.

    For this reason a man shall leave his father and his mother
        and be joined to his wife,
    and the two shall become one flesh.

This is a great mystery,
        but I speak in reference to Christ and the Church.

The word of the Lord.   **Response:** *Thanks be to God.*

Selection NT-7 (Philippians 4:4-9)

A reading from the Letter of Saint Paul to the Philippians.

Brothers and sisters:
Rejoice in the Lord always.
I shall say it again: rejoice!
Your kindness should be known to all.
The Lord is near.
Have no anxiety at all, but in everything,
     by prayer and petition, with thanksgiving,
     make your requests known to God.
Then the peace of God that surpasses all understanding
     will guard your hearts and minds in Christ Jesus.

Finally, brothers and sisters,
     whatever is true, whatever is honorable,
     whatever is just, whatever is pure,
     whatever is lovely, whatever is gracious,
     if there is any excellence
     and if there is anything worthy of praise,
     think about these things.
Keep on doing what you have learned and received
     and heard and seen in me.
Then the God of peace will be with you.

The word of the Lord.   **Response:** *Thanks be to God.*

Selection NT-8 (Colossians 3:12-17)

A reading from the Letter of Saint Paul to the Colossians.

Brothers and sisters:
Put on, as God's chosen ones, holy and beloved,
     heartfelt compassion, kindness, humility, gentleness, and
       patience,
     bearing with one another and forgiving one another,
     if one has a grievance against another;
     as the Lord has forgiven you, so must you also do.
And over all these put on love,

that is, the bond of perfection.
And let the peace of Christ control your hearts,
    the peace into which you were also called in one Body.
And be thankful.
Let the word of Christ dwell in you richly,
    as in all wisdom you teach and admonish one another,
    singing psalms, hymns, and spiritual songs
    with gratitude in your hearts to God.
And whatever you do, in word or in deed,
    do everything in the name of the Lord Jesus,
    giving thanks to God the Father through him.

The word of the Lord.   **Response:** *Thanks be to God.*

Selection NT-9 (Hebrews 13:1-4a, 5-6b)

A reading from the Letter to the Hebrews.

Brothers and sisters:
Let mutual love continue.
Do not neglect hospitality,
    for through it some have unknowingly entertained angels.
Be mindful of prisoners as if sharing their imprisonment,
    and of the ill-treated as of yourselves,
    for you also are in the body.
Let marriage be honored among all
    and the marriage bed be kept undefiled.
Let your life be free from love of money
    but be content with what you have,
    for he has said, *I will never forsake you or abandon you.*
Thus we may say with confidence:

    The Lord is my helper,
    and I will not be afraid.

The word of the Lord.   **Response:** *Thanks be to God.*

James L. Shaffer

Selection NT-10 (1 Peter 3:1-9)

A reading from the first Letter of Saint Peter.

Beloved:
You wives should be subordinate to your husbands so that,
    even if some disobey the word,
        they may be won over without a word by their wives'
            conduct
        when they observe your reverent and chaste behavior.
Your adornment should not be an external one:
    braiding the hair, wearing gold jewelry, or dressing in fine
            clothes,
    but rather the hidden character of the heart,
    expressed in the imperishable beauty
    of a gentle and calm disposition,
    which is precious in the sight of God.
For this is also how the holy women who hoped in God
    once used to adorn themselves
    and were subordinate to their husbands;
        thus Sarah obeyed Abraham, calling him "lord."
You are her children when you do what is good
    and fear no intimidation.

Likewise, you husbands should live with your wives in
            understanding,
    showing honor to the weaker female sex,
    since we are joint heirs of the gift of life,
    so that your prayers may not be hindered.

Finally, all of you, be of one mind, sympathetic,
    loving toward one another, compassionate, humble.
Do not return evil for evil, or insult for insult;
    but, on the contrary, a blessing, because to this you were
called,
    that you might inherit a blessing.

The word of the Lord.   **Response:** *Thanks be to God.*

Selection NT-11 (1 John 3:18-24)

A reading from the first Letter of Saint John.

Children, let us love not in word or speech
    but in deed and truth.

Now this is how we shall know that we belong to the truth
    and reassure our hearts before him
    in whatever our hearts condemn,
    for God is greater than our hearts and knows everything.
Beloved, if our hearts do not condemn us,
    we have confidence in God
    and receive from him whatever we ask,
    because we keep his commandments and do what pleases him.
And his commandment is this:
    we should believe in the name of his Son, Jesus Christ,
    and love one another just as he commanded us.
Those who keep his commandments remain in him, and he in them,
    and the way we know that he remains in us
    is from the Spirit that he gave us.

The word of the Lord.   **Response:** *Thanks be to God.*

Selection NT-12 (1 John 4:7-12)

A reading from the first Letter of Saint John.

Beloved, let us love one another,
    because love is of God;
    everyone who loves is begotten by God and knows God.
Whoever is without love does not know God, for God is love.
In this way the love of God was revealed to us:
    God sent his only-begotten Son into the world
    so that we might have life through him.
In this is love:
    not that we have loved God, but that he loved us
    and sent his Son as expiation for our sins.
Beloved, if God so loved us,
    we also must love one another.

No one has ever seen God.
Yet, if we love one another, God remains in us,
    and his love is brought to perfection in us.

The word of the Lord.   **Response:** *Thanks be to God.*

Selection NT-13 (Revelation 19:1, 5-9a)

A reading from the Book of Revelation.

I John, heard what sounded like the loud voice
    of a great multitude in heaven, saying:
        "Alleluia!
    Salvation, glory, and might belong to our God."
A voice coming from the throne said:
        "Praise our God, all you his servants,
        and you who revere him, small and great."
Then I heard something like the sound of a great multitude
    or the sound of rushing water or mighty peals of thunder,
    as they said:
        "Alleluia!
    The Lord has established his reign,
        our God, the almighty.
    Let us rejoice and be glad
        and give him glory.
    For the wedding day of the Lamb has come,
        his bride has made herself ready.
    She was allowed to wear
        a bright, clean linen garment."
(The linen represents the righteous deeds of the holy ones.)
Then the angel said to me,
    "Write this:
    Blessed are those who have been called
    to the wedding feast of the Lamb."

The word of the Lord.   **Response:** *Thanks be to God.*

Alleluia Verse and Verse Before the Gospel

Selection AV-1 — 1 John 4:7b

Everyone who loves is begotten of God and knows God.

Selection AV-2 — 1 John 8b, 11

God is love.
If God loved us, we also must love one another.

Selection AV-3 — 1 John 4:12

If we love one another,
God remains in us
and his love is brought to perfection in us.

Selection AV-4 — 1 John 4:16

Whoever remains in love,
remains in God and God in him.

Gospel Readings

Selection G-1 (Matthew 5:1-12a)

Priest/Deacon: A reading from the holy Gospel according to Matthew.
Response: Glory to you, Lord.

When Jesus saw the crowds, he went up the mountain,
    and after he had sat down, his disciples came to him.
He began to teach them, saying:
       "Blessed are the poor in spirit,
           for theirs is the Kingdom of heaven.
       Blessed are they who mourn,
           for they will be comforted.
       Blessed are the meek,
           for they will inherit the land.
       Blessed are they who hunger and thirst for righteousness,
           for they will be satisfied.
       Blessed are the merciful,
           for they will be shown mercy.
       Blessed are the clean of heart,
           for they will see God.
       Blessed are the peacemakers,
           for they will be called children of God.
       Blessed are they who are persecuted for the sake of
               righteousness,
           for theirs is the Kingdom of heaven.
       Blessed are you when they insult you and persecute you
           and utter every kind of evil against you falsely because of me.
       Rejoice and be glad,
           for your reward will be great in heaven."

The Gospel of the Lord.   **Response:** *Praise to you, Lord Jesus Christ.*

Selection G-2 (Matthew 5:13-16)

Priest/Deacon: A reading from the holy Gospel according to Matthew.
Response: Glory to you, Lord.

Jesus said to his disciples:
"You are the salt of the earth.

But if salt loses its taste, with what can it be seasoned?
It is no longer good for anything
    but to be thrown out and trampled underfoot.
You are the light of the world.
A city set on a mountain cannot be hidden.
Nor do they light a lamp and then put it under a bushel basket;
    it is set on a lamp stand,
        where it gives light to all in the house.
Just so, your light must shine before others,
        that they may see your good deeds
        and glorify your heavenly Father."

The Gospel of the Lord.   **Response:** *Praise to you, Lord Jesus Christ.*

Selection G-3 — Long Form (Matthew 7:21, 24-29)

Priest/Deacon: *A reading from the holy Gospel according to Matthew.*
Response: *Glory to you, Lord.*

Jesus said to his disciples:
"Not everyone who says to me, 'Lord, Lord,'
    will enter the Kingdom of heaven,
    but only the one who does the will of my Father in heaven.

"Everyone who listens to these words of mine and acts on them
    will be like a wise man who built his house on rock.
The rain fell, the floods came,
    and the winds blew and buffeted the house.
But it did not collapse; it had been set solidly on rock.
And everyone who listens to these words of mine
    but does not act on them
    will be like a fool who built his house on sand.
The rain fell, the floods came,
    and the winds blew and buffeted the house.
And it collapsed and was completely ruined."
When Jesus finished these words,
        the crowds were astonished at his teaching,
        for he taught them as one having authority,
        and not as their scribes.

The Gospel of the Lord.   **Response:** *Praise to you, Lord Jesus Christ.*

Selection G-3 — Short Form (Matthew 7:21, 24-25)

Priest/Deacon: *A reading from the holy Gospel according to Matthew.*
Response: *Glory to you, Lord.*

Jesus said to his disciples:
"Not everyone who says to me, 'Lord, Lord,'
    will enter the Kingdom of heaven,
    but only the one who does the will of my Father in heaven.

"Everyone who listens to these words of mine and acts on them
    will be like a wise man who built his house on rock.
The rain fell, the floods came,
    and the winds blew and buffeted the house.
But it did not collapse;
    it had been set solidly on rock."

The Gospel of the Lord.   **Response:** *Praise to you, Lord Jesus Christ.*

Selection G-4 (Matthew 19:3-6)

Priest/Deacon: *A reading from the holy Gospel according to Matthew.*
Response: *Glory to you, Lord.*

Some Pharisees approached Jesus, and tested him, saying,
    "Is it lawful for a man to divorce his wife for any cause
        whatever?"
He said in reply, "Have you not read that from the beginning
    the Creator *made them male and female and said,*
    For this reason a man shall leave his father and mother
    and be joined to his wife, and the two shall become one flesh?
So they are no longer two, but one flesh.
Therefore, what God has joined together, man must not separate."

The Gospel of the Lord.   **Response:** *Praise to you, Lord Jesus Christ.*

Selection G-5 (Matthew 22:35-40)

Priest/Deacon: *A reading from the holy Gospel according to Matthew.*
Response: *Glory to you, Lord.*

One of the Pharisees, a scholar of the law, tested Jesus by asking,
    "Teacher, which commandment in the law is the greatest?"

He said to him,
> "You shall love the Lord, your God,
> with all your heart,
> with all your soul,
> and with all your mind.

This is the greatest and the first commandment.
The second is like it:
> You shall love your neighbor as yourself.

The whole law and the prophets depend on these two
> commandments."

The Gospel of the Lord.   **Response:** *Praise to you, Lord Jesus Christ.*

Selection G-6 (Mark 10:6-9)

Priest/Deacon: *A reading from the holy Gospel according to Mark.*
Response: *Glory to you, Lord.*

"From the beginning of creation,
> *God made them male and female.*

For this reason a man shall leave his father and mother
> *and be joined to his wife,*
> *and the two shall become one flesh.*

So they are no longer two but one flesh.
Therefore what God has joined together,
> no human being must separate."

The Gospel of the Lord.   **Response:** *Praise to you, Lord Jesus Christ.*

Selection G-7 (John 2:1-11)

Priest/Deacon: *A reading from the holy Gospel according to John.*
Response: *Glory to you, Lord.*

There was a wedding in Cana in Galilee,
> and the mother of Jesus was there.

Jesus and his disciples were also invited to the wedding.
When the wine ran short,
> the mother of Jesus said to him,
> "They have no wine."

And Jesus said to her,
> "Woman, how does your concern affect me?

My hour has not yet come."
His mother said to the servers,
    "Do whatever he tells you."
Now there were six stone water jars there for Jewish ceremonial
        washings,
    each holding twenty to thirty gallons.
Jesus told them,
    "Fill the jars with water."
So they filled them to the brim.
Then he told them,
    "Draw some out now and take it to the headwaiter."
So they took it.
And when the headwaiter tasted the water that had become wine,
        without knowing where it came from
        (although the servants who had drawn the water knew),
        the headwaiter called the bridegroom and said to him,
        "Everyone serves good wine first,
        and then when people have drunk freely, an inferior one;
        but you have kept the good wine until now."
Jesus did this as the beginning of his signs in Cana in Galilee
        and so revealed his glory,
        and his disciples began to believe in him.

The Gospel of the Lord.   **Response:** *Praise to you, Lord Jesus Christ.*

Selection G-8 (John 15:9-12)

Priest/Deacon: *A reading from the holy Gospel according to John.*
Response: *Glory to you, Lord.*

Jesus said to his disciples:
"As the Father loves me, so I also love you.
Remain in my love.
If you keep my commandments, you will remain in my love,
    just as I have kept my Father's commandments
    and remain in his love.

"I have told you this so that my joy might be in you
    and your joy might be complete.
This is my commandment: love one another as I love you."

The Gospel of the Lord.   **Response:** *Praise to you, Lord Jesus Christ.*

Selection G-9 (John 15:12-16)

Priest/Deacon: *A reading from the holy Gospel according to John.*
Response: *Glory to you, Lord.*

Jesus said to his disciples:
"This is my commandment: love one another as I love you.
No one has greater love than this,
    to lay down one's life for one's friends.
You are my friends if you do what I command you.
I no longer call you slaves,
    because a slave does not know what his master is doing.
I have called you friends,
    because I have told you everything I have heard from my
        Father.
It was not you who chose me, but I who chose you
    and appointed you to go and bear fruit that will remain,
    so that whatever you ask the Father in my name he may give
        you."

The Gospel of the Lord.   **Response:** *Praise to you, Lord Jesus Christ.*

Selection G-10 — Long Form (John 17:20-26)

Priest/Deacon: *A reading from the holy Gospel according to John.*
Response: *Glory to you, Lord.*

Jesus raised his eyes to heaven and said:
"I pray not only for my disciples,
    but also for those who will believe in me through their word,
    so that they may all be one,
    as you, Father, are in me and I in you,
    that they also may be in us,
    that the world may believe that you sent me.
And I have given them the glory you gave me,
    so that they may be one, as we are one,
    I in them and you in me,
    that they may be brought to perfection as one,
    that the world may know that you sent me,
    and that you loved them even as you loved me.
Father, they are your gift to me.

I wish that where I am they also may be with me,
>that they may see my glory that you gave me,
>because you loved me before the foundation of the world.
Righteous Father, the world also does not know you,
>but I know you, and they know that you sent me.
I made known to them your name and I will make it known,
>that the love with which you loved me
>may be in them and I in them."

The Gospel of the Lord.   **Response:** *Praise to you, Lord Jesus Christ.*

Selection G-10 — Short Form (John 17:20-23)

Priest/Deacon: *A reading from the holy Gospel according to John.*
Response: *Glory to you, Lord.*

Jesus raised his eyes to heaven and said:
"Holy Father, I pray not only for these,
>but also for those who will believe in me through their word,
>so that they may all be one,
>as you, Father, are in me and I in you,
>that they also may be in us,
>that the world may believe that you sent me.
And I have given them the glory you gave me,
>so that they may be one, as we are one,
>I in them and you in me,
>that they may be brought to perfection as one,
>that the world may know that you sent me,
>and that you loved them even as you loved me."

The Gospel of the Lord.   **Response:** *Praise to you, Lord Jesus Christ.*

James L. Shaffer

Rite of Marriage

The Rite of Marriage

Questions to the Couple

Priest: My dear friends, you have come together in this church so that the Lord may seal and strengthen your love in the presence of the Church's minister and this community. Christ abundantly blesses this love. He has already consecrated you in baptism and now he enriches you by a special sacrament so that you may assume the duties of marriage in mutual and lasting fidelity. And so, in the presence of the Church, I ask you to state your intentions.

N. and N., have you come here freely and without reservation to give yourselves to each other in marriage?

Bride and Groom: I have.

Priest: Will you love and honor each other as man and wife for the rest of your lives?

Bride and Groom: I will.

Priest: Will you accept children lovingly from God, and bring them up according to the law of Christ and his Church?

Bride and Groom: I will.

Priest: Since it is your intention to enter into marriage, join your right hands, and declare your consent before God and his Church.

The Giving of Consent (Vows)

Selection V-1

Groom: I, N., take you, N., to be my wife. I promise to be true to you in good times and in bad, in sickness and in health. I will love you and honor you all the days of my life.

Bride: I, N., take you, N., to be my husband. I promise to be true to you in good times and in bad, in sickness and in health. I will love you and honor you all the days of my life.

Priest: You have declared your consent before the Church. May the Lord in his goodness strengthen your consent and fill you

both with his blessings.
What God has joined, men must not divide.
Response: *Amen.*

Selection V-2

Groom: I, N., take you, N., for my lawful wife, to have and to hold, from this day forward, for better, for worse, for richer, for poorer, in sickness and in health, until death do us part.
Bride: I, N., take you, N., for my lawful husband, to have and to hold, from this day forward, for better, for worse, for richer, for poorer, in sickness and in health, until death do us part.
Priest: You have declared your consent before the Church. May the Lord in his goodness strengthen your consent and fill you both with his blessings.
What God has joined, men must not divide.
Response: *Amen.*

Selection V-3

Priest: N., do you take N., to be your wife? Do you promise to be true to her in good times and in bad, in sickness and in health, to love and honor her all the days of your life?
Groom: I do.
Priest: N., do you take N., to be your husband? Do you promise to be true to him in good times and in bad, in sickness and in health, to love and honor him all the days of your life?
Bride: I do.
Priest: You have declared your consent before the Church. May the Lord in his goodness strengthen your consent and fill you both with his blessings.
What God has joined, men must not divide.
Response: *Amen.*

Selection V-4

Priest: N., do you take N., for your lawful wife, to have and to hold, from this day forward, for better, for worse, for richer, for

poorer, in sickness and in health, until death do you part?
Groom: I do.

Priest: N., do you take N., for your lawful husband, to have and to hold, from this day forward, for better, for worse, for richer, for poorer, in sickness and in health, until death do you part?
Bride: I do.

Priest: You have declared your consent before the Church. May the Lord in his goodness strengthen your consent and fill you both with his blessings.

What God has joined, men must not divide.
Response: Amen.

The Blessing of Rings

Selection BR-1

Priest: May the Lord bless ✠ these rings which you give to each other as the sign of your love and fidelity.
Response: Amen.

Selection BR-2

Priest: Lord,
bless these rings which we bless ✠ in your name.
Grant that those who wear them
may always have a deep faith in each other.
May they do your will
and always live together
in peace, good will, and love.
[We ask this] through Christ our Lord.
Response: Amen.

Selection BR-3

Priest: Lord,
bless ✠ and consecrate N. and N.
in their love for each other.
May these rings be a symbol
of true faith in each other,

and always remind them of their love.
Through Christ our Lord.
Response: *Amen.*

The Bestowal of the Rings

Groom / Bride:
N., take this ring as a sign of my love and fidelity. In the name of the Father, and of the Son, and of the Holy Spirit. Amen.

Prayer of the Faithful

During this part of the Mass, which is also known as the General Intercessions, the Church offers prayers to God on behalf of its needs and concerns. Usually, at a wedding liturgy, we pray for the Church and its leaders, for married couples, and for all those present. This would be a fine opportunity to offer prayers for people who have been important to your lives and to your faith, such as Godparents or Confirmation sponsors. You may also wish to remember those members of your families who have died, or who are ill. Please let the priest or deacon know about any special intentions, and if you would like a member of the congregation to be the reader. Two sample Prayers of the Faithful are provided below. The priest or deacon may be able to suggest other prayers of intercession or assist in composing a suitable prayer of your own.

A. Priest / Deacon:
On this joyous occasion, we call to mind God's many blessings, and we ask him to hear our prayers.

Reader:

The response to each prayer is: Lord, hear our prayer.
1. For Pope N. , our Bishop N. and all those who lead the Church on earth, we pray to the Lord.

R. Lord, hear our prayer.

2. For N. and N. who are united in Matrimony this day, that God may help them to live as true partners in life and love, we pray to the Lord.

R. Lord, hear our prayer.

3. For all married couples and families, that the Lord may guide and protect them in all moments of life, we pray to the Lord.

R. Lord, hear our prayer.

4. For the sick and suffering, that we may be a sign of God's compassion to them, we pray to the Lord.

R. Lord, hear our prayer.

5. For those who have died, and especially for the deceased members of the families and friends of the bride and the groom (in particular for...), we pray to the Lord.

R. Lord, hear our prayer.

Priest / Deacon:
Loving Father, we ask you to hear our prayers and to bless all those united in Matrimony, that we may always know of your mercy and love for us. We ask this through Jesus Christ, our Lord.
R. Amen.

B. Priest / Deacon:
At this celebration of Christ's presence to us in the sacraments, we present our petitions before our Heavenly Father.

Reader:
The response to each prayer is: Lord, bless your people.
1. For all the leaders of God's Holy Church, we pray to the Lord.

R. Lord, bless your people.

2. For the newly married couple, N. and N. , and for all couples united in Matrimony, we pray to the Lord.

R. Lord, bless your people.

3. For a greater respect for human life, at all stages of its development, from conception until natural death, we pray to the Lord.

R. Lord, bless your people.

4. For an increase in true devotion and in living the call to love one another as Christ has loved us, we pray to the Lord.

R. Lord, bless your people.

5. For those who are ill, lonely, frightened, or in trouble, that God may give them comfort by our lives, we pray to the Lord.

R. Lord, bless your people.

6. For those who have died, and especially for the deceased loved ones of the bride and the groom, we pray to the Lord.

R. Lord, bless your people.

Priest / Deacon:
Loving God, we come before you as your trusting children who desire to live in your love. Grant that we may accept your will as we present our needs to you, in the name of your Son, our Lord, Jesus Christ.
R. Amen.

Presentation of the Gifts

At this time, members of the congregation bring to the altar the bread and wine to be used for the celebration of the Eucharist. Many brides and grooms ask their parents, or other close family members, to represent the Church community by bringing up these gifts.

Liturgy of the Eucharist

Prayer over the Gifts

Selection PG-1

Priest: Lord,
accept our offering
for this newly-married couple, N. and N.
By your love and providence you have brought them together;
now bless them all the days of their married life.
[We ask this] through Christ our Lord.

Response: Amen.

Selection PG-2

Priest: Lord,
accept the gifts we offer you
on this happy day.
In your fatherly love,
watch over and protect N. and N.,
whom you have united in marriage.
[We ask this] through Christ our Lord.

Response: Amen.

Selection PG-3

Priest: Lord,
hear our prayers
and accept the gifts we offer for N. and N.
Today you have made them one in the sacrament of marriage.
May the mystery of Christ's unselfish love,
which we celebrate in this Eucharist,
increase their love for you and for each other.
[We ask this] through Christ our Lord.

Response: Amen.

Gene Plaisted, OSC

Eucharistic Prayer

The Eucharistic Prayer is the most solemn part of the Mass. The Church has several prayers that can be used. They can be found in any Sunday missal. Each of these is a beautiful, but varied, expression of the reality of the Eucharist and our relationship with God. If you wish the priest to use one of these prayers in particular, please discuss it with him.

Nuptial Blessing

Selection NB-1

My dear friends, let us turn to the Lord and pray
that he will bless with his grace this woman [or N.],
now married in Christ to this man [or N.]
and that [through the sacrament of the body and blood of Christ]
he will unite in love the couple he has joined in this holy bond.

Father, by your power you have made everything out of
        nothing.
In the beginning you created the universe
and made mankind in your own likeness.
You gave man the constant help of woman
so that man and woman should no longer be two, but one flesh,
and you teach us that what you have united
may never be divided.

Father, you have made the union of man and wife so holy a
mystery
that it symbolizes the marriage of Christ and his Church.

Father, by your plan man and woman are united,
and married life has been established
as the one blessing that was not forfeited by original sin
or washed away in the flood.

Look with love upon this woman, your daughter,
now joined to her husband in marriage.

She asks your blessing.
Give her the grace of love and peace.
May she always follow the example of the holy women
whose praises are sung in the scriptures.

May her husband put his trust in her
and recognize that she is his equal
and the heir with him to the life of grace.
May he always honor her and love her
as Christ loves his bride, the Church.

Father, keep them always true to your commandments.
Keep them faithful in marriage
and let them be living examples of Christian life.
Give them the strength which comes from the gospel
so that they may be witnesses of Christ to others.
[Bless them with children
and help them to be good parents.
May they live to see their children's children.]
And, after a happy old age,
grant them fullness of life with the saints
in the kingdom of heaven.
We ask this through Christ our Lord.

Response: Amen.

Selection NB-2

Let us pray to the Lord for N. and N.
who come to God's altar at the beginning of their married life
so that they may always be united in love for each other
[as now they share in the body and blood of Christ].

Holy Father, you created mankind in your own image
and made man and woman to be joined as husband and wife
in union of body and heart
and so fulfill their mission in this world.

Father, to reveal the plan of your love,

you made the union of husband and wife
an image of the covenant between you and your people.

In the fulfillment of this sacrament,
the marriage of Christian man and woman
is a sign of the marriage between Christ and the Church.
Father, stretch out your hand, and bless N. and N.

Lord, grant that as they begin to live this sacrament
they may share with each other the gifts of your love
and become one in heart and mind
as witnesses to your presence in their marriage.
Help them to create a home together
[and give them children to be formed by the gospel
and to have a place in your family].

Give your blessings to N., your daughter,
so that she may be a good wife [and mother],
caring for the home,
faithful in love for her husband,
generous and kind.

Give your blessings to N., your son,
so that he may be a faithful husband
[and a good father].

Father, grant that as they come together to your table on earth,
so they may one day have the joy of sharing your feast in heaven.
We ask this through Christ our Lord.

Response: *Amen.*

Selection NB-3

My dear friends, let us ask God
for his continued blessings upon this bridegroom and his bride [or
N. and N.].

Holy Father, creator of the universe,
maker of man and woman in your own likeness,
source of blessing for married life,
we humbly pray to you for this woman

who today is united with her husband in this sacrament of marriage.

May your fullest blessing come upon her and her husband
so that they may together rejoice in your gift of married love
[and enrich your Church with their children].

Lord, may they both praise you when they are happy
and turn to you in their sorrows.
May they be glad that you help them in their work
and know that you are with them in their need.
May they pray to you in the community of the Church,
and be your witnesses in the world.
May they reach old age in the company of their friends,
and come at last to the kingdom of heaven.

We ask this through Christ our Lord.

Response: Amen.

Guidelines for the Reception of Communion

For Catholics

As Catholics, we fully participate in the celebration of the eucharist when we receive holy communion. We are encouraged to receive communion devoutly and frequently. In order to be properly disposed to receive communion, participants should not be conscious of grave sin and normally should have fasted for one hour. A person who is conscious of grave sin is not to receive the Body and Blood of the Lord without prior sacramental confession except for a grave reason where there is no opportunity for confession. In this case, the person is to be mindful of the obligation to make an act of perfect contrition, including the intention of confessing as soon as possible (Code of Canon Law, canon 916). A frequent reception of the sacrament of penance is encouraged for all.

For Fellow Christians

We welcome our fellow Christians to this celebration of the eucharist as our brothers and sisters. We pray that our common baptism and the action of the Holy Spirit in this eucharist will draw us closer to one another and begin to dispel the sad divisions that separate us. We pray that these will lessen and finally disappear, in keeping with Christ's prayer for us "that they may all be one" (John 17:21).

Because Catholics believe that the celebration of the eucharist is a sign of the reality of the oneness of faith, life, and worship, members of those churches with whom we are not yet fully united are ordinarily not admitted to holy communion. Eucharistic sharing in exceptional circumstances by other Christians requires permission according to the directives of the diocesan bishop and the provisions of canon law (canon 844 § 4). Members of the Orthodox Churches, the Assyrian Church of the East, and the Polish National Catholic Church are urged to respect the discipline of their own churches. According to Roman Catholic discipline, the Code of Canon Law does not object to the reception of communion by Christians of these churches (canon 844 § 3).

For Those Not Receiving Holy Communion

All who are not receiving holy communion are encouraged to express in their hearts a prayerful desire for unity with the Lord Jesus and with one another.

For Non-Christians

We also welcome to this celebration those who do not share our faith in Jesus Christ. While we cannot admit them to holy communion, we ask them to offer their prayers for the peace and the unity of the human family.

James L. Shaffer

Special Devotions

After Communion, there is usually a brief period for meditation and prayer. This can be done in silence, or it may be accompanied by music.

The bride and groom occasionally use this period for special devotions, such as presenting a bouquet of flowers at the altar of Our Lady, or the lighting of a marriage candle. If you desire to do any special devotions at this time, please consult with the priest or deacon.

Prayers After Communion

Selection PC-1

Lord,
in your love
you have given us this Eucharist to unite us with one another
and with you.
As you have made N. and N.
one in this sacrament of marriage
[and in the sharing of the one bread and the one cup],
so now make them one in love for each other.

We ask this through Christ our Lord.

Response: Amen.

Selection PC-2

Lord,
we who have shared the food of your table
pray for our friends N. and N.,
whom you have joined together in marriage.
Keep them close to you always.
May their love for each other

proclaim to all the world
their faith in you.

We ask this through Christ our Lord.

Response: *Amen.*

Selection PC-3

Almighty God,
may the sacrifice we have offered
and the Eucharist we have shared
strengthen the love of N. and N.,
and give us all your fatherly aid.
We ask this through Christ our Lord.

Response: *Amen.*

RITE OF CONCLUSION

Solemn Blessings at the End of Mass

Selection SB-1

God the eternal Father keep you in love with each other,
so that the peace of Christ may stay with you
and be always in your home.

Response: *Amen.*

May [your children bless you,]
your friends console you
and all men live in peace with you.

Response: *Amen.*

May you always bear witness to the love of God in this world
so that the afflicted and the needy
will find in you generous friends,
and welcome you into the joys of heaven.

Response: *Amen.*

And may almighty God bless you all,
the Father, and the Son, ✠ and the Holy Spirit.

Response: Amen.

Selection SB-2

May God, the almighty Father,
give you his joy
and bless you [in your children].

Response: Amen.

May the only Son of God have mercy on you
and help you in good times and in bad.

Response: Amen.

May the Holy Spirit of God
always fill your hearts with his love.

Response: Amen.

And may almighty God bless you all,
the Father, and the Son, ✠ and the Holy Spirit.

Response: Amen.

Selection SB-3

May the Lord Jesus, who was a guest at the wedding in Cana,
bless you and your families and friends.

Response: Amen.

May Jesus, who loved his Church to the end,
always fill your hearts with his love.

Response: Amen.

May he grant that, as you believe in his resurrection,
so you may wait for him in joy and hope.

Response: Amen.

And may almighty God bless you all,
the Father, and the Son, ✠ and the Holy Spirit.

Response: Amen.

Selection SB-4

May almighty God, with his Word of blessing, unite your hearts in the never-ending bond of pure love.

Response: Amen.

May your children bring you happiness, and may your generous love for them be returned to you, many times over.

Response: Amen.

May the peace of Christ live always in your hearts and in your home.

Response: Amen.

May you have true friends to stand by you, both in joy and in sorrow.
May you be ready and willing to help and comfort all who come to you in need.
And may the blessings promised to the compassionate be yours in abundance.

Response: Amen.

May you find happiness and satisfaction in your work. May daily problems never cause you undue anxiety, nor the desire for earthly possession dominate your lives. But may your heart's first desire be always the good things waiting for you in the life of heaven.

Response: Amen.

May the Lord bless you with many happy years together, so that you may enjoy the rewards of a good life. And after you have served him loyally in his kingdom on earth, may he welcome you to his eternal kingdom in heaven.

Response: Amen.

And may almighty God bless you all,
the Father, and the Son, ✠ and the Holy Spirit.

Response: Amen.

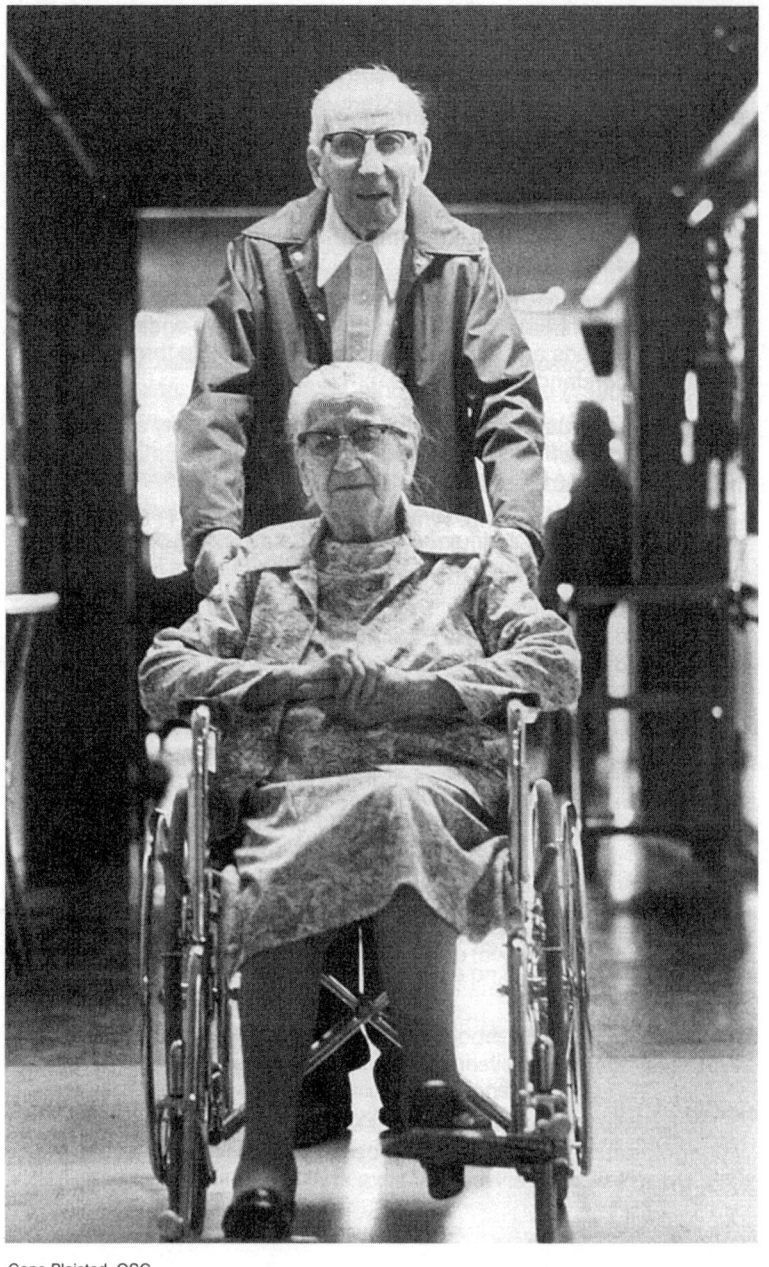

Gene Plaisted, OSC

Afterword

Monsignor John G. Woolsey

Director of the Family Life/Respect Life Office of the Archdiocese of New York 1979-1996

The Christian Sacrament of Matrimony is a real sign of God's grace expressed in the unconditional love shared between a husband and wife. The Catholic Church conceives marriage as the intimate partnership of life and love which has been established by God and endowed by Him with its proper nature, laws and gifts. Church teaching mirrors the New Testament's development of marriage, through which Christ himself established the Sacrament of Matrimony.

Jesus proclaims the nature of Christian marriage when His opponents, trying to trick Him, ask Him about the difficult problem of divorce. He calls His questioners back to the truth of the beginning of creation to stress that the covenant between man and wife is marked by life-long fidelity and love (Matthew 19:4-5). Jesus is radical and prophetic in His response. He emphasizes the faithfulness of God — and of marriage. In Jesus' perspective, the idea of marriage as a unity or bond between a man and a woman anchors the action of God who creates humanity in His image as male and female. Jesus' prohibition of divorce highlights the teaching of the Jewish prophets — God loves His Chosen People as a husband loves his wife; God's heart is pure, not hard; and His love is faithful and enduring. "'I hate divorce,' says the LORD God of Israel" (Malachi 2:16).

Saint Paul also gives fresh insight into the dynamic intimacy of the marriage bond. Paul perceives that a Christian man or woman consecrates an unbelieving spouse in their conjugal union (1 Corinthians 7:14). Paul's wisdom flowers in his Letter to the Ephesians, which describes the marriage of Christian men and women. In Ephesians 5:22-

30, Paul emphasizes that husband and wife are interdependent in their self-giving love for each other. In Ephesians 5:31-32 the teaching of Genesis shines in a new light: "For this reason a man shall leave his father and mother and shall cling to his wife, and the two shall be made into one. This is a great foreshadowing; I mean that it refers to Christ and the Church." The conjugal union then is not only natural, it is profoundly spiritual, for its identity takes root within the body of Christ.

From this we see various levels of meaning in marriage. Jesus underscores the sacred nature of marriage between a man and a woman whom God created in His image and likeness and whom God joins to become two in one flesh. Paul sees another level of sacramentality in the marriages of those whom Jesus Christ incorporated and in whom the Spirit lives.

The foundation of each level of meaning is the intimate partnership of life and love which the Second Vatican Council states that marriage is. Marriage is truly and profoundly an interpersonal relationship in which a man and a woman share their lives in a permanent, faithful and fruitful union beginning with their marriage vows and continuing throughout their married life.

Marriage preparation programs seek to help a couple who plan to marry. The goal is to help them to develop and deepen their interpersonal relationship and to heighten their awareness of its sacramental meaning. This handbook, significantly entitled *Partners in Life and Love*, is intended to provide men and women preparing for their life together with a concise presentation of the teaching of the Church on the Sacrament of Holy Matrimony. The discussion of marriage, the selection of scripture readings and the liturgical guide are available to help engaged couples and those preparing them for the celebration of matrimony to learn about their faith and properly prepare for the rite of marriage. The couples will then, with God's grace, become ministers of a marriage which reflects their love for each other as well as God's love for them and for us in the community of the Church.

Suggested Readings

1. Catholic Belief and Doctrine

Catechism of the Catholic Church (especially paragraphs 1601 to 1666 on the Sacrament of Marriage)

On Human Life (Humanae Vitae), Pope Paul VI

On the Family (Familiaris Consortio), Pope John Paul II

Letter to Families, Pope John Paul II

Christian Family in the Teachings of John Paul II, Pope John Paul II (Alba House 1990) — A small paperback containing the teachings of the Holy Father on family life and living.

Human Sexuality: A Catholic Perspective for Education and Lifelong Learning, United States Catholic Conference (1990)

Marriage: The Rock on Which the Family is Built, William F. May (Ignatius Press 1995) — A leading Catholic theologian discusses Church teaching on marriage and sexuality.

What God Has Joined: The Sacramentality of Marriage, Msgr. Peter J. Elliott (Alba House 1990) — A member of the Pontifical Council for the Family discusses marriage as a sacrament of the Church.

2. Christian Marriage in General

God at Work: Christian Marriage and Family for Partners and Parents, Philip Cody (St. Paul 1993) — Insights into practical issues of marriage, with a warm and positive spiritual approach.

A Catholic Handbook for Engaged and Newly Married Couples, Frederick W. Marks (Faith Publishing 1994) — Conservative advice on practical and spiritual issues.

Marriage is Love Forever, James Socias (Scepter Publishers 1994) —Traditional presentation of Catholic belief and practice.

Read the Fine Print Before You Say "I Do", Jack Leipert (Paulist Press 1994) — Light pastoral advice on building a strong married relationship.

Loving Against the Odds, Rob Parsons (Hodder & Stoughton 1994) — Not specifically Catholic, but a Christian approach to marriage, very good on building relationship skills.

Courage to Love... When Your Marriage Hurts, Gerald Foley (Ave Maria Press 1992) — Based on experiences from marriage restoration ministry, offers excellent advice on how to save a hurting marriage.

The Catholic Wedding Book, Molly K. Stein and William C. Graham (Paulist Press 1988) — Practical advice about planning a wedding given in a humorous and light manner.

3. Communication and Relationships in General (this topic is also covered in many of the books listed under "Christian Marriage" above)

If Only He Knew, Gary Smalley (Harper Paperbacks 1979) — Excellent practical advice for husbands to better understand their wives and to strengthen their relationship through that understanding.

For Better or Best, Gary Smalley (Harper Paperbacks 1979) — Excellent practical advice for wives to better understand their husbands and to strengthen their relationship through that understanding.

4. Christian Sexuality (Catholic approaches to sexuality are also included in most of the books listed under "Christian Marriage" above; the following are additional resources)

Natural Family Planning: Why It Succeeds, Herbert F. Smith, S.J. (Pauline Books and Media 1995) — An excellent introduction to Natural Family Planning.

Intimate Bedfellows: Love, Sex, and the Catholic Church, Thomas and Donna Finn (St. Paul Books and Media 1993) — A light and humorous discussion of sexuality from a Catholic perspective.

Courage to Love, Mary Shivanandan (KM Associates 1979) — A discussion of what Natural Family Planning can bring to a marriage, as well as important issues for couples practicing NFP.

Instructions: Read through the selections on pages 6 through 7. When you have made your choices, write them on the lines below. Bring this form with you when you speak to your priest or deacon to plan your wedding ceremony.

Bride: _____

Groom: _____

Best Man: _____

Maid of Honor: _____

Date of Wedding: _____   Time: _____

Date of Rehearsal: _____   Time: _____

Opening Prayer: Selection Number: OP- _____ Page: _____

Old Testament Reading: Selection Number: OT- _____ Page: _____

                                Reader: _____

Responsorial Psalm: Selection Number: RP- _____ Page: _____

                                Reader: _____

New Testament Reading: Selection Number: NT- _____ Page: _____

                                Reader: _____

Alleluia Verse: Selection Number: AV- _____ Page: _____

Gospel: Selection Number: G _____ Page: _____

The Giving of Consent (Vows):   Selection Number: V- _____ Page: _____

Blessing of Rings: Selection Number: BR- _____ Page: _____

                                One Ring: _____ Two Rings: _____

Prayer of the Faithful: _____

Special Intentions: _____

_____

_____

_____

Reader: _____

Presentation of the Gifts: Presenters: _____

_____   _____

_____   _____

Prayer over the Gifts: Selection Number: PG- _____ Page: _____

Eucharistic Prayer: Prayer Number: _____

Nuptial Blessing: Selection Number: NB- _____ Page: _____

Receiving Communion: Bride: _____ Groom: _____

Host only: _____ Both Species: _____

Special Devotions: _____

_____

_____

Prayer After Communion: Selection Number: PC- _____ Page: _____

Solemn Blessing: Selection Number: SB- _____ Page: _____

Notes: _____

_____

_____

_____

_____

_____